ASTROLOGY FOR BEGINNERS

HOW TO LEARN ASTROLOGY, THE COMPLETE MANUAL TO DISCOVERY HOROSCOPE AND ZODIAC SIGNS

DAVID HOFFMAN

Table of Contents

INTRODUCTION

While astrology is not a religion, it provides warmth, trust, and a more fundamental understanding of the world we reside in.

Interpretations also provide guarantees of one's future, but more specifically, they are meant to show us a way to solve our problems and strengthen our partnership with our spouses, the families, and mates and, above all, opportunities to explore and experience our own inner worlds in a different light.

Astrology believes nothing in existence is coincidental and everything that happens to us occurs for a specific reason. Astrology may give us some good answers as to why these things are happening to us, and it guides us in our growth. Astrology also helps people understand themselves and the world around them much better in this way. Astrology is important, and not astrologers. Most people who visit astrologers or regularly read their horoscopes end up feeling a sense of happiness and excitement a little like euphoria.

This does not mean that astrologers have accurately predicted potential or current individuals based on their horoscope times, but it does mean that getting a horoscope set will potentially be a very fulfilling experience. The Planet is located under the constellations that were recognized as the signals of our planets millennia ago. Although the signals no longer align with the constellations, we are still under the control of seasons and celestial motions in the same manner as we were back then.

Most individuals closely observe their horoscopes and trust in the significance of their astrology signs. This is not surprising, as astrology is widely popular, and everyone in the world knows what their horoscope dates and signs are. People enjoy reading their future via horoscope signs and this often contributes to shifts in attitudes, habits and the processes of decision making. Astrology can be a total lifesaver, as it helps you to know future obstacles and issues in advance.

It's up to you whether you want to follow the suggestions and measures provided by reading a horoscope and save yourself from suffering without doing much. Here's your first question. There's no "without doing a thing" redemption. This is the main problem with the solution of map readings–everyone has to make a strong effort to change things in their lives.

Some people believe in astrology because others have done it before them, and curiosity is the basic human nature, but the more astrology is drawn, the clearer things become. The days of the zodiac, the signals. We should connect zodiac signs with almost any aspect of our lives, and we will see that they are genuinely wise and right. Our horoscopes are special and can help us find and show our talents, shortcomings and natural attributes. Astrology can also help us find out which marriages are compatible-and which are not. Horoscope compatibility will boost our partnership with other zodiac signs.

Through understanding the capacity for love, you will make the most of the possibilities and take the appropriate steps that contribute to a healthy marriage. Astrology takes into consideration two foundational pillars-our capacity for conception, as well as the effects of planets and stars on our personal horoscope. This can help us choose the right course of career and education to make a decent and successful life.

Last but not least, we believe in astrology because it's about us. My horoscope is like a map of my future that was created when I was born. It ensures that my birth map is almost as rare as my fingerprints. The placement of every planet in my horoscope can reveal a lot about my personality and destiny.

Astrocartography is a form of position astrology that attempts to identify different living conditions by variations in geographical location. Reportedly, by applying your birth map to different parts of the world, you will decide the region where you will be most effective.

CHAPTER ONE:
Major Facts About Astrology

The terms horoscope and astrology were the two things most searched on the Internet, as shown in a 2014 survey.

Astrology is known to be both an art, and a science. Astrology is art, as it involves research to draw the various aspects together and to gain a better understanding of the personality traits of the individual. Sixtus IV became the first Catholic pope to establish and interpret a horoscope; Leo X and Paul III both relied on astrologers for direction, while Julius II astrologically chose his coronation date.

Adolf Hitler, Nazi Germany's leader, found astrology quite significant. The German emperor is believed to have met with astrologers throughout the Second World War.

Exploring the Planets in Astrology

The word "planets" as used in Astrology does not mean only the planets in the Solar System, but the entirety of the celestial bodies that exist in the Solar System. The Sun and the Moon are two lights in everyone's natal chart, having a greater effect on us than any sun, and are a star and the satellite of the Earth. Neither should we ignore the impact of some asteroids nor did dwarf planets, particularly now that Pluto was downgraded to the status of a dwarf planet and still rules Scorpio's sign.

It has been debated that Ceres shows similar qualities of the Virgo sign, although this has yet to be decided in the astrological study of the future. Each celestial body's position in a horoscope is a real projection to the ecliptic of its current position in space. That being said, we must always bear in mind that there are no realistic signs of the Zodiac.

Relative to the Sun, the Earth, and all other bodies in the Solar System, we often use Lunar Nodes in our conceptions as a simple metaphor for karmic behavior and the creation of one's Soul. These are described as points in trajectories and planets (Planetary Nodes) of Moon (Lunar Nodes), where the ecliptic intersects.

The Planets

In order to really appreciate how each planet should be viewed in any astrological analysis, we need to see each of them as a specific entity with positive and negative characteristics. We don't understand the sides and those who represent us well or even make us feel excited. Although in our simple conceptions each of the planets and lights speaks to different objects, colors or numbers. We grasp them better by our implicit interaction with them. Through one of the philosophical approaches, it is said that if there were no relationships in our lives, there would be no one to bear witness to our existence. If we had no relationships, we would have gone away from a sample that defines what is.

Through our partnerships, we are all pretty well established, and the whole Zodiac system is made up of oppositions we have had to overcome in this lifetime. Planets appear to be there only to capture entire personalities and characters, so we can use the general knowledge to describe our inner states and relationships. Growing planet governs one or two signs in the Zodiac system, and the signs they govern are best described as concentrated energies on all planets. We will see them as individuals further colored by the signs in which they are placed, and their dignity will talk about their ability to grow roots in a certain position and give their best to enrich our lives.

In order to truly understand astrology, you will need to find a way to truly understand whoever appears in your life, regardless of the difficulty in your relationship. Each planet will obviously be well understood in your own chart, and finally you will be at peace with the world and ready to share your knowledge with others.

If you are still in conflict or have trouble forgiving someone in your life, think of your customers as working partners who will give as much as they get. That astrological appointment is a lesson for both parties involved, and you should never ignore the impact on your life that this planet sitting before you has. Comprehension of the significance of aspects and their role in our analysis is crucial for any reading when it comes to astrological interpretations of any kind. Without them, we can only sense an aura or know the attributes of a person, but we cannot grasp the interactions they have in their life, their parents' relationships, and the relational ties that distinguish them.

When you have found the birth map to be a schematic depiction of your genes, we can see that things are identical to ties between two DNA molecules.

Aspects

An aspect reflects one of the unique angles created in a zodiac sphere by representations of various celestial bodies, house cusps, or imaginary points. Their key role is to make our map fluid, reflect relationships between different bodies and demonstrate the flow of time by orbs and planetary velocity.

Each aspect is a point of view, a point of view, and how one celestial body looks at the other. If an aspect is positive and easy, energy will flow, and we will see the entities involved looking at each other with love, admiration, or just support and acceptance. Only by raising awareness and recognizing more energy is needed to repair what is missing or heal wounds left to our identity will stress seen through challenging aspects be resolved.

When we consider every celestial body as an individual with a certain function in our lives, we will see its presence in a sign reflects the task itself, the house in which it is representing the place or the region of life where it occurs and manifestations, and aspects reflect the relationships it has formed.

We will see the biggest polarization with other people comes from jumping into squaring or opposing positions in our charts, depending on the role we decide to take ourselves. Keep in mind there is no such thing as a "right moment in time" when all stars are synchronized to display the energy flow equilibrium. If there wasn't something we need to know on our path to enlightenment, we wouldn't be here on planet Earth, because obstacles are the key to it. While easy people with many positive aspects in their chart have enough simplicity and consistency in their life, they will often lose the deep inner drive force and the need to battle for new successes if they have no problems to overcome.

That's why we see so many individuals with "good charts" struggling to do something meaningful with their lives, while those most troubled prefer to use their challenges' unchecked strength to guide it in a path that makes them happy. In our road to joy, those of us who have to struggle for fulfillment always leap a step further than those who have already been raised a little better, and in the larger order of things we all have our important roles.

Ptolemaic Aspects

Modern astrology recognizes many angular relationships as minor aspects, but in every interpretation, we have to separate those with a long tradition and a fundamental role from those with less noticeable manifestations. Identified as "Aspects of Ptolemy," such five primary partnerships are represented as angles of 0, 60, 90, 120 and 180 degrees in one map. Several astrologers find the partnerships of 30° and 150° to be nearly as important as the rest of these because they seem to represent two missed points in the circle's 30-by-30 division. Nonetheless, the major features seen and described by Ptolemy by conventional astrology are always the following:

Conjunction

A conjunction is a 0-degree dimension, with a permissible orb up to 17 degrees if the Sun is involved.

This talks of one's self and has optimistic as well as harmful connotations, based on the existence of the entities involved. We will see the conjunction as challenging for this planet if there is a malefic pressing on another planet, especially if its dignity is low. On the other side, if a beneficent planet is a part of the combination, it will be viewed as a supportive dimension in conjunction with the supporting planet, particularly for a malefic.

They must bear in mind that "positive and negative stars" do not exist. The individual experience and the way we look at them is the only thing that poses a difficulty. So, from our point of view, Saturn is maleficent, dark and pushing us out of the shadows, but this is just a part of human nature that pushes us to avoid assuming responsibility, having trouble dealing with unconscious energies that we would rather reject.

Saturn is our deepest faith in its most positive glow, our relationship with God and our ability to take our lives into our hands, being a grown-up, capable, strong, with clear boundaries. Likewise, one's Venus can be sweet, caring, lovely, or in a manner that is evil, transforming us into gluttony, laziness, or adultery. It's all about interpretation.

A special case of a conjunction that we need to be mindful of is called the Cazimi conjunction, and only the Sun can do it. It is an exact alignment that occurs no more than 16 minutes into the star, and the planet that lies very close to the Sun is said to be "in the Sun's center" or "in the King's hands." This is a stance that refers to the world in question about a favor because it is shielded by the highest god-the star who gives us life.

Opposition

Opposing entities form an aspect in 180 degrees, and this puts them on two furthest points in the zodiacal circle. - Critiques speaks about "The Others" and the challenge of accepting differences we have with other individuals. The opposition's main challenge is to accept that completely different things have a common point in common, and that each sign in the Zodiac appears to simply mirror the one across. Any conflict is common ground to see who we are in detail, and instead of shifting blame, looking for shortcomings in everyone else and competing with others to reach the point of equality, we have to accept our differences and understand that what really disturbs us in other individuals is our own flaws.

Branches of Astrology

There are 6 branches explained in this book.

The understanding of astrology has evolved since ancient times, as people interpreted the location of the stars in relation to agricultural needs and told stories about the fireplace inspired by the sky. It has developed over time, as an extremely powerful tool for self-discovery and all sorts of predictions, in many different directions, to meet different needs of humanity.

Astrology was everything from a voting device for the kings, to a ray of optimism for those in need. This turns out that it was always affected by its dark ages and decay in a good way, for now it's better than ever, with so many different things to sell and various solutions to meet any need that comes to mind. The Basics Division of Astrology would locate Modern Astrology in the Western Hemisphere and call it Western Astrology, while the East will mostly be synonymous with Vedic, or Indian Astrology.

Most of these have evolved separately and they differ greatly in their basic presumptions, as well as their astronomical points of interest, charts and divisions. First of all, Indian Astrology uses sidereal Zodiac, while Western Astrology is based on the tropical Zodiac defined by the early spring period. Sidereal Zodiac is bound to a set star Spica, which is known to be the exact opposite of Aries' beginning. This star is currently located in the tropical zodiac around the 24th degree of Libra, making a difference of about 24 degrees between those zodiacs. These two zodiacs are going to be identical once in every 25,920 years, and the next match will not take place for thousands of years to come.

Western Astrology

Most of our emphasis will be centered on Western Astrology divisions, as it provides the best insight into a human being as an adult, with strengths and weaknesses, leaving room for temperament and situations change in life. It would be rough to say that Western Astrology is closest to freewill, but it leaves more room than other astrological teachings for changing one person's destiny.

Eastern astrologers also assert right to the creation of astrology itself, hanging on to the constants of the Zodiac that underpin all of their scheme. The problem with this approach resides mostly in the argument itself, since nobody owns astrology and there is no "true astrology," only the one every astrologer knows best. Simply put, if we want to think things are not set in stone, we're going to turn our heads to the left and find comfort, psychological reasons, and hope for improvement in the West just as we'd find acceptance, compromise, and dignity in the North. Modern astrology acknowledges several different branches inside, and it's not easy to list them all. There may be other, unlisted solutions out there and while most of them are included here or come under one of these definitions, some might have actually slipped our minds.

Relationship Astrology

Astrology can also be used not only to describe the cause of a person, but also to consider his or her relationship with a totally different human being. We use Relationship Astrology to consider the middle ground between two (or more) individuals, their potential problems and places where the energy flow is quick and peaceful.

Connections in the Zodiac

This type of astrology is commonly used not because of magic of love and romance but also because relationships are what really determines our inner being. The entire Zodiac circle consists of oppositions, which speak of 6 types of relationships that have 12 signs of the Zodiac.

Each element is a relationship itself, and each layout they have should show them colors and shades as well as their added diversity. Without partnerships we wouldn't be alive, and we would not be here at all, because they don't come to us and to other men, but also to our interactions with our souls, Heart and soul.

Others are just our own mirror and they're going to talk about our inner conditions and stuff we love or problems we're having difficulty solving, the way we see them. Anything affects us in others is a large part of our own nature, and we should keep this in mind every second of the way, in every confrontation we have to overcome.

Techniques and Horoscopes in Marriage Astrology, as in all other types of Astrology, we must remain aware that nothing can manifest between two individuals unless it is already depicted in the two different birth charts.

We need to delegate positions to each person we want to research our partnership with and see from our own map what their aim is, where do we interact, how do they support us in this lifespan, and how do we help them.

Synastry

In order to study the partnership between two men, we usually compare their charts first through synastry. This is a method of matching two birth maps with all their celestial birth locations, homes and features. If we see that the world in one map has an identical feature of the planet in the other chart, we realize this is an important link between these entities. The more facets we share, the more we benefit from our connection, the greater the role each planet can play.

So, we'll expect aspects of a romantic relationship between Venuses or strong contact through sexual links between the Moon and Mars, Venus and Mars, or between Mars and Mars. In synastry, it will be important to look at the arrangements in each other's chart. It implies that if one person has a planet in a certain symbol, we understand the importance of the role of the other individual as the ruler of that sign. This is the planet that will lead the first to its specific dignity and aspects.

For starters, the best scenario would be to see two friends, one in Capricorn with the Moon and the other in Taurus with Saturn. It would mean that their wife tells the first person to find love inside and form the values of home and family that are totally lacking.

Composite Charts- When we make the first touch between two people via synastry, we shift to the composite map of their partnership.

There are two forms of comparative maps, the first being the Midpoint form (all celestial locations are the logical center of human birth positions) and the Davison or the Time and Space system (all positions are true for the same middle time between births). The main difference between these two maps is the manner in which they are made, the first being a set of hypothetical points in space that describe how the partnership is perceived, and the second a list of actual positions for the middle period that identify the true object resided by two individuals. Combined, they're going to give us a snapshot of a relationship as a third person that holds two individuals together, and the way it's viewed and treated, as well as where it actually leads.

Feminine and Masculine Planets

Most of us survive through archetypes consumed by our culture and the degree of awareness of our entire human race. It is impossible to completely escape the definition of masculine and feminine types, even though we all have both sides hiding within. In most cases, when we interpret relationships between individuals of opposite sex, each of them will play the role of their respective planets and lights, meaning that the female partners will be presented to Moon and Venus, just as the male partners will play the role of the Sun and Mars.

Some of us will be asexual in this context if our role overcomes the archetype, so a female teacher with a significant teaching role will often be introduced to Jupiter, even though he mostly speaks of Zeus and the masculine principle within. Or maybe a male artist could take on the role of Venus with a little more ease. This is analogous to how we look at children by Mercury, a world of both sexes and mental asexuality.

In the case of same-sex relationships, particularly intimate ones, an astrologer will have to ask specific questions to determine if the spouse tends to take on a task. In this case, we will usually be led by the older partner as the one who shows a little more masculine quality, and by a personal description that fits a certain planet or light into a certain sign.

Financial Astrology

Financial astrology does not have the same meaning in different parts of the world, even though its purpose always promotes the financial well-being of an individual or a group. In the United States, this is a division used to assess the movement of the stock market and the state of the economy as a whole, while in countries which do not have a high standard, it tends to consult and advice on the making of money and the economy of a person, their business, or simply offers a worldly view of the financial situation in the country.

In the United States, this division is also called Business Astrology or Economic Astrology, and it is one of the most common divisions used and often practiced by non-astrologers to enforce their financial decisions. Schools and lectures are increasingly available, and many economists who have to manage risky investments choose to rely on advice from a professional astrologer using this branch.

Financial Astrology in Other Countries

Lower standards and a different approach to the economy in different countries of the world do not make it possible to use this approach linked to the stock market. Although the word will mostly be used for this specific purpose in Financial Astrology, we have to recognize that there are financial astrologers who simply work for people, their career paths or their businesses. In the above approach, this division will intermingle with Electoral Astrology to assess a company's best possible time to start, make investments or take out a loan.

From such a viewpoint, we might conclude that the Financial Astrology branch is simply part of Natal Astrology, because it literally focuses emphasis on one particular area of life, but it doesn't really share the same purpose. While Natal Astrology will focus on increasing the overall awareness of the individual, helping to make major life changes in the direction of one's evolution, Financial astrology should adhere to the houses and signs of the Earth dimension, focusing primarily on practical issues contributing to the customer's material satisfaction.

While thinking about these two methods we should bear in mind that their phases and use are very different. Though Financial Astrology "Wall Street" gives unalterable circumstances and a basic "go-with - the-flow" means of implementation. Some strategies are versatile and will allow the client to choose right time for electoral action, help anticipate potential events and make room for personal improvement that will lead to a change in finances.

Energy Astrology

Another of the divisions of astrology that arrived in the 21st century with its creation is the another that links the celestial bodies with our chakra.

Energy Astrology is based on the assertion that each planet and light we use in our basic astrological approach corresponds to one of the chakras, while all the signs and houses simply add their color to the story of the planets.

Basic Principles

There are seven heavenly bodies that can be seen by the naked eye in the night sky (or by day when we speak of the sun). In Energy Astrology, each one of them shows the flow of energy in one of our energy centers–the chakras. The first chakra, or root chakra, will be linked to Mars, and from someone's chart we can find out where the problem lies in its position, dignity and aspects. The more complicated one place becomes; the more energy will be obstructed, and its flow disrupted. In reality, it's amazing how these items are interconnected.

When you test how the lack of balance presents itself in one of the chakras and equate it with the lack of balance that the accompanying world holds, you'll be surprised to find that they function in complete contrast. So, if we see that someone has their Mars in a difficult location, as astrologers, we can instantly understand that this individual has an issue with force, anxiety and violence, and these are all representations of a problem at the level of the first chakra.

Benefits

The positive side of this strategy is that it offers us more space for recovery. Work in the field of energy is quite traditional in Eastern medicine, and the path to bioenergy treatment has many adherents from all walks of life and from all over the planet. If nothing is really extreme, we can all at least calm our body and pay special attention to the spasm in the place where the chakra is situated. The greatest thing that this approach to astrology has to bring is the relation it brings to our physical body.

Because most of the other parts dwell on thinking, logical analysis, and understanding of one's life and character, Energy Astrology will remind us that we are all humans, made of flesh and bone, and that we have to take care of our physical needs first. This is a subset assisted by contemplation and calming methods of all sorts, as well as the traditional astrology of the Natal Map, which will provide us a method for understanding basic astrological details and help us identify various dignities and roles.

PSYCHOLOGICAL ASTROLOGY

Although Astrology is this wide field of fantastic meaning, the way it influences our psychological state and the depths of our minds can be quite surprising. Even since Carl Jung established an archetypal link between symbols and already established psychological phenomena, many open-minded psychologists have tried his approach. It has been found over time that this relation between a theory and a "pseudoscience," which they like to term astrology, can be rendered very scientifically.

Connection Astrology and Psychology have been linked in many ways, but the most common and important is the connection with Natal Astrology. Although it is the basis for almost every other astrological branch, it plays a particularly important role here, as it clarifies some of the problems that the client may have before the point of personal understanding and dialog is reached. While predictive approaches are seldom used in this methodology, mostly because of the significance of the psychological field to astrologers, they will come in handy once the root of the problem is identified and the causes for its expression can be anticipated.

Balance

The biggest challenge this division has to address is to strike a balance between the two, as it is done by individuals who are diversely trained. It offers an immense potential to work for customers and with anyone's selves as well, but only if both "sciences" are used fairly and their importance is apparent from any point of view.

Through the point of view of astrology, and the thrill of the incredible situations and deep understanding of the Cosmos that it offers, psychology may seem to be so rigid or constrained by human race standards. On the other side, something as rooted and practical as Psychology also treats Astrology as a little more of a sport and takes away its interest. The secret to a successful relationship between the two resides in a genuine passion for both, and it's not that hard to come by if you really want to find meaning in the depths of your mind.

Dreams

The beautiful meaning of every fantasy you've ever heard of is clarified magnificently by astrology. Sadly, we are too often presented with the simplistic understanding of dreaming, and this takes away the true meaning of dreams and our path through our subconscious mind. While we don't notice, the greatest archetypal symbolism is centered right here.

If you get acquainted with both viewpoints on any subject that is being replicated in your life, it will be an immense relief to explore the trends that make it happen in the first place. The solution to any problem ahead rests in our ability to solve what we have already been through, and if we treat our existence as this beautiful calculation, this section of Astrology will allow us to learn two factors in advance.

MEDICAL ASTROLOGY

For order to truly grasp what Medical Astrology is, we need to understand the connection between different parts of the body to each other and how the entire system of our body functions.

Medical astrology is focused on the association of each body part and organ with a certain meaning and, as such, fits very well with energy astrology.

Elements

In the use of Medical Astrology, we have to keep in mind that our body is one entire structure, rather than dividing it into many pieces, but still maintain our attention on specific things that could emerge as physical conditions owing to celestial locations. The most important thing to consider is the context of each object when we start drawing conclusions about someone's health and intensity.

Any physical condition and our propensity to cause the issue to go deeper is always connected to the dimension of Earth. For order for any question to reach the level of our physical body, it must be ignored while it was on our mental and emotional flights. This is especially true of the health conditions that require surgery and the removal of some bodily part. Although this may sound odd, any surgical procedure talks of unchangeable factors, problems we could not overcome, yet finally pushed far enough into our unconscious, where they had to show themselves as a foreign body within our own.

Organs

Organs in our body has their own role, as well as a certain astrological picture is known. Such meaning is treated differently, and sometimes you have difficulty identifying which world governs the organ and why. For example, our heart is connected to the Sun and the Moon at the same time, and it won't always be easy to see where the health problem comes from. Note that our aim in Medical Astrology is not specifically to point to the part of the body in question, but to identify possible problems in their heart and to find a way to overcome them. Our main goal is to balance our clients and help them find a way to revive the symbolism of lost, fallen and finally found planets. It is our responsibility to shift them from the point of frustration that contributed to their disease in the first place, and to make room for personal growth in order to overcome this.

EVOLUTIONARY ASTROLOGY

Evolutionary Astrology is a philosophy that places our Soul at the center and allows us to learn what this life on planet Earth holds as our teacher, and what we have been through before we were born. This is one of the most enigmatic of all the divisions of Astrology, mainly because it focuses mostly on regeneration to begin with and presupposes that our Soul has a direction to go in many lifetimes. Nevertheless, there is another perspective that helps us to incorporate this element of our philosophical theory, since it can also be seen as a path of the Soul through many layers of our subconscious and unconscious mind

Practice

In general, this section is described using the Jeffrey Wolf Green process. In its basic assumptions, this approach is descriptive, and what distinguishes it from many others is its insistence on how to address one important question – why? It gives us the chance to value one's Self, our Existence, and its future, which helps to separate human desire from the growth potential and development.

By this theory, we are all on the way to reconnect with the energy of the Universal Source, and our bodies represent lifetimes with certain steps along this path. This division is often used in conjunction with Behavioral Astrology and past life trauma counseling, rendering it one of the most important divisions of all human psyche. Evolution may literally be seen as personal growth.

Planetary Positions

Evolutionary Astrology focuses on Pluto and the Lunar Nodes, as representations of our earlier incarnations and our relation to the "underworld," our inner planet, or the past, whatever the term. Each birth chart will be viewed in relation to these forces, and every specific world will be a point of connection to them. Very often this division is related to the use of an equivalent house system, a need apparently similar to karmic astrology and to the themes of Saturn or Pluto.

In this type of reading, our chart will be a tool to add color to the story behind the Nodes, combined with Pluto and its location in the house and the sign. Pluto is the main actor here, because it reflects the needs of the Soul that have yet to be met, contributing to the search for fulfillment of unhealthful wishes that cannot come to life, liberating themselves from them, and going through an unconscious process of transformation that brings us closer to the Cosmos itself.

CHAPTER TWO:
Zodiac Elements

For a deeper understanding of Astrology, there are four elements of nature we shall consider in this section, they are: Earth, Water, Fire and Air. These four elements have been identified and put in use as well long before our own time. The Alchemist made use of them in their search for answers while the common people used them in the quest for understanding Nature, these four elements have proven to be the pillar of all that we are surrounded by and even everything that we are made up of.

ZODIAC AND THE ELEMENTS

All the four elements speak extensively of certain probabilities possessed by each zodiac sign as it belongs to each one of them.

They help us to properly understand that there are different ways through which we view each individual around us. As it gives us the needed patience in dealing with those that have traits that differ from ours. Also, it gives us a reason to understand why it is some of these signs are compatible with some than the others. In a general interpolation, the element of

Earth will go perfectly well with Water, and Fire will go well with Air. Logical thinking makes this less complicated, for the element of Water gives the element of Earth its fertility which brings us to life, while the element of Air keeps the element Fire alive (burning) and ignites the light and our strength of creation.

Natural Order of Things

If we observe this division of the various elements in a bigger picture, we will be able to readily agree that without any of these elements, life would not be a possibility as they are all equally important to our very own existence here on earth. Naturally, they sync with each other perfectly, constantly working together daily.

Their separation into the higher and lower energies is only a major reflection of the very vital need of the human race dividing into two distinct compartments – the good and the bad, emotion and reason, masculine and feminine, plus and minus and so on. I would want you as you decide whatever it is you do with what you read in this book, to have it at the back of your mind that none of these elements has a greater worth than the other in any way, you must also have it in mind that all these elements have one major thing in common – matter.

This is an indestructible link which connects them all to make up the image we have of our physical body, which is densely represented by the element of Earth. Without the element of Earth, life in this physical form that we have it today would not have been made possible and you would be without those major senses you possess in form of tasting, touching, smelling, and even hearing.

This goes to say that the manifestation of all these aforementioned senses depend greatly on the element of Earth, and that being said, the element of Earth possess to be the most difficult to which a substitute can be made available for in one's natal chart when it is not positioned strongly.

Interpretation of Elements

As soon as you have the opportunity of appraising someone's natal chart, the position occupied by each element should be your first and major interest. If upon seeing the position of each element you get to see that such an individual has no planets present in one of them, you have successfully identified a very wide, but very particular problem that such individual has to proffer solution to during his or her lifetime.

The absence of planets in any one of the elements in a person's natal chart speaks loudly of the inability of the person to efficiently connect with it. This can in turn result in problems on all other planes of existence, as it is evident that all of the four elements have to work together as one in order for us to create anything true and significant in our lives here on earth. However, when the situation is entirely opposite and an individual has many planets in only one of the elements, this situation makes it be hard to slow down things, strike a balance in this plane with all the other ones and also remain in a peaceful state.

Special Planets

There can also be the advent of a very special situation where a person has just one of the planets in one of the elements, especially if the planet is among one of the lights or visible planets.

This situation will appear to be that of a drowning man who has just one straw at his disposal and he is holding on to it strongly as though it is his only way out.

The Element of Air

That is the element this binds all elements. However, due to its invisibility, it sometimes appears to be less significant. The distance from Earth's nature lifts us high in impractical and mental planes that does not meet our physical needs. Now, this is the element that can be found in all others, holding the fire going just as the hydrogen burns in the Sun. We might say the beginning of life wouldn't be possible without Fire, but without Air there wouldn't be a Fire on our world. The dimension of Air allows us room to breathe, widens our lungs and opens our Soul to personal liberty with them. All the signs which belong to this dimension have a strong need to feel free and liberated.

Air Signs

The Gemini, Libra and Aquarius are signs that depict the dimension of Air in the Zodiac. Ironically, two of them have a problem with the Sun, Libra causing it to fall and Aquarius to the downside of it. This is understandable for the Sun holds everything in balance and circles around it, and instead, Air must be free to orbit the Earth. Looking at the larger picture, people born under the strong influence of these signs have a problem fitting into a regular order of their surroundings, regardless of whether it is their country or their place of work. Their main goal in life is often simply to stop pleasing others and to worry about their opinions, so that they can follow their brightest and most liberating ideas.

How Then Do We Balance Air?

For each person marked by Air the biggest challenge is finding balance and understanding the importance of their body. Within higher realms, where everything is simpler and seems probable, they have a clear tendency to stay.

Finding a way to transform their thoughts, intelligence and knowledge into practical things and truly make them alive is not easy. The most important thing for Airy individuals to really succeed in personal growth and overall development is to stop talking and start making concrete, practical moves towards fulfilment.

They are balanced by the Earth element, and need a healthy daily routine, with their meals repeated every day at the same time, and physical activity to remain conscious of their physical existence. For example, if they fail to eat, this void in their stomach will affect every reasonable strategy they have had. The value of fulfilling their physical requirements is fundamental and irreplaceable.

The Element of Fire

When thinking about the Fire factor, we need to bear in mind this is the only element that shines. Water can sparkle, that's real, but only if it reflects the light produced by Fire as a massive, fiery celestial body, whether a campfire or the Sun.

This is the element that reflects energy itself, and although the element of Water contains a lot of earthly energy, it cannot be contrasted with the amount of energy that resides in the Sun, although it may be equally important to the human race.

Fire Signs

In the Zodiac, the aspect of Fire is represented by Aries, Leo, and Sagittarius. Such signs really elevate the power of the Sun and each born person has an assignment to cultivate and cherish their emotional side as one of these Sun signs. We often have to be prepared for compassion and a deeper understanding of other people, and they have fundamental problems in relationships that are caused by their need to give something to those who have not asked for anything.

Every fiery individual has to use their energy solely in their own lives, unless someone asks for advice and commitment. Of all three, Sagittarius is the most gifting, for they're at the end of this Fire trine, which has already gained so much, with a clear philosophy of life and many good intentions.

The Gemini, Libra and Aquarius are signs that depict the dimension of Air in the Zodiac. Ironically, two of them have a problem with the Sun, Libra causing it to fall and Aquarius to the downside of it. This is understandable for the Sun holds everything in balance and circles around it, and instead, Air must be free to orbit the Earth.

Looking at the larger picture, people born under the strong influence of these signs have a problem fitting into a regular order of their surroundings, regardless of whether it is their country or their place of work. Their main goal in life is often simply to stop pleasing others and to worry about their opinions, so that they can follow their brightest and most liberating ideas.

This is the first item with strong masculine energy and it easily neglects the feminine values within, burning everything around a person and evaporating all the Water in their body and life. A life without love is not worth living, and all the fiery people have to value their emotional side and consider their emotional needs to make them happier. This translates into their relationship with women in the outer world, suppressing the feminine principle on a wider scale, leading to all sorts of conflicts which ultimately take human life.

For anyone guided by the element of Fire the biggest challenge is to stay calm and peaceful along the way. People born in Fire with an ascendant or many planets tend to forget that passive approach is just as much needed as active approach with a strong need to move forward. Therapy could do miracles here, because when they learn something new and get an opportunity to save or recycle some of their waste energy, they don't lack awareness or excitement.

The Element of Water

This is the dimension of constant movement, but slow and steady, flowing within each of us and maintaining the mystery of each. This is the element of conception and death, illusions and fairy tales which hold our Soul's secret-its beginning and its end.

We're literally dealing with life and death issues, our genetic inheritance and all our ancestors in the element of Water. Strangely enough, that too is the dimension of emotions. We must all understand that somebody in our family tree has already lived through our emotions, and they are passed down from generation to generation, mostly through the role of the mother.

Water Signs

Cancer, Scorpio and Pisces are indications belonging to the elements of Air. It renders the whole need for this dimension a little confusing, since Cancer's ruler lies in Scorpio, and Pisces seems to be there to cover his body. Perhaps this is the hardest challenge of all, embracing the bad as much as the good, anger and sadness as much as compassion for each of us to welcome feeling. Typical Air element representatives have often been said to be overly emotional.

Once they know there's no such thing they will deal with a lot of pain. Their flexibility and fragile nature make them perfect for psychologists and caring clinicians, supporting those with profound emotional issues. They came to this planet to teach everybody else that love is truly endless, and is our greatest quality feelings.

How Then Do We Balance Water?

People with a Water accent have something to learn about their emotional character. This is the element of greatest possibilities but often puts us to sleep and makes it impossible for an individual to express themselves creatively. This is a world of all strengths, and all that we have left in this lifespan to carry.

The element of Fire burns bright as a guiding light, and gives energy, passion, and direction to the person where they can find their talents and use them through creation. The Element of Water standing alone and simply carries us from shore to shore, from left to right, and while life may be magical and dreamy within it, we could simply spin in circles without finding any way out.

The Element of Earth

Earth's element is the sole purpose of all elements, as it is the basis for each of them, for our existence, and something we all want to accomplish-materializing our desires. This is a somewhat difficult element because it is static and unmovable, particularly when an individual has plenty of planets in it, but not enough of them in the Air aspect to even it out. This is our planet's dimension and got its name from it, too. We will bear this in mind when reading anyone's charts, because the lack of Earth could point to big problems a person finds grounding or connecting to the soil to which they were born.

EARTH SIGNS

Signs governed by the Earth element are the Taurus, Virgo, and Capricorn. It is immediately apparent that these are all practical signs that value material things, work hard and know how to make a plan and put it into action.

All three have the ability to be specific and concrete, expecting everyone else to share their world view and reasonable approach. World is matter itself, our physical body, our wealth, the food we eat and our daily routine. Strongly set in their ways, individuals with this accented dimension tend to give in for years to an unchanging pattern, sometimes too scared to get out of it. In a challenging mode, they will stick to habits that don't make them happy just because they're convinced, they have to, or stay at a job due to financial security, while neglecting their intelligence and creativity altogether

How Then Do We Balance Earth?

Earth's biggest challenge is realizing something as strong, fragile and transparent as Air. Earthlings out of sync need to throw off their restrictive patterns, make unrepentant adjustments to their lives and schedule, and stop questioning any choice they have already made. Their sense of purpose must be transparent and their interaction with intense and unshakeable feelings, and that requires a special commitment for someone like Virgo to carry Venus into decline.

Such individuals will read to get in contact with the dimension of Air, have a coffee break, wander aimlessly and socialize as much as possible. We need a spoken word instead of a written one, a modern device, people who change places and goals to show them how to travel, and plenty of rest and relaxing to brace their bodies for the transition. For anyone under pressure from Earth the best exercise is dancing, spontaneous and carefree, with modern loud music and preferably with a relaxed partner.

CHAPTER THREE:
The Twelve Zodiac Signs

The Zodiac's twelve signs are divided into four elements — fire, earth, air, and water. Each of these elementary groupings has distinct characteristics. Together, they shape the natural world, so that each is in some way dependent on the other.

Fire Signs: Aries, Leo, Sagittarius

Earth Signs: Taurus, Virgo, Capricorn

Air Signs: Gemini, Libra, Aquarius

Water Signs: Cancer, Scorpio, Pisces

The Fire Signs: Aries, Leo, Sagittarius

Fire signals, like fire itself, appear to be intense, complex and wild. Fire may keep you warm, or it can do a great deal of destruction. Although fire burns rapidly without fuel to keep it burning, it can also regain its strength from the ashes. A single spark can set fire to the forest.

As a consequence, fire signals need to be properly monitored and handled.

The Air Signs: Gemini, Libra, Aquarius

Air signs are all about movement, thoughts, and motion — they're the "winds of transition." When a big gust strikes you,

you can't help but run. While some may be true-life "airheads" within their ranks, others are as strong as the G-force of gravity. Air signals offer everyone a breath of fresh air as things start to slow down. Like the wind, you can't catch them all, and you never know where they're going to dump you once they're going to sweep you free. It's almost always an adventure, however.

The Earth Signs: Taurus, Virgo, Capricorn The Earth signals are keeping it real. We are the "established" people on the planet, the ones that carry us down to Earth and encourage us to begin with a solid foundation. Slow and steady, these "masters" are faithful and strong, and we hold to their citizens during hard times. We are realistic on good days; at worst, we can be materialistic or too concentrated on the surface of things to dive into the deep.

The Water Signs: Intuitive, emotional and ultrasensitive water signs can be as mysterious as the ocean itself. They can be cool, like wind, or they can trap you in their depths. Such signs often have vivid hallucinations and borderline-psychic intuitions.

Security is important to them — after all, water needs a jar, or it dries up and vanishes. 6 of these zodiac signs are explained below:

AQUARIUS ZODIAC SIGN

Aquarius Characteristics: Strengths: progressive, original, autonomous, compassionate weaknesses: psychological, stubborn, uncompromising, unapproachable

Aquarius likes: fun with friends, helping others, fighting for causes, intelligent conversation, good listening

Aquarius dislikes: Constraints, empty promises, loneliness, dull or boring circumstances, Aquarius-born people that disagree with them are quiet and shy, but in the other hand they could be eccentric and heavy.

In both instances, though, they are deep thinkers and highly intellectual people who love supporting others. They can see without prejudice, on both sides, that makes them people who can easily solve problems. Although they can quickly adjust to the energies that affects them, the Aquarius-born need to be alone for some time and away from everything in order to restore strength.

Aquarius is an air symbol, and as such, he utilizes his imagination at every moment. If there is no intellectual stimulus, they're lazy, and they're not inspired to get the best result. Uranus, the founding planet of Aquarius, has a shy, blunt and sometimes violent disposition, but it also brings imaginative qualities to Aquarius.

You are aware of seeing the future, so you know exactly what they want to do five or ten years from now. Uranus has also granted them the ability of swift and quick change, so that they are recognized as philosophers, socialists, and humanists. The biggest problem with Aquarius-born is the sense that they are confined or restricted.

Because of their desire for freedom and dignity for all, they will always seek to guarantee freedom of speech and movement. They will always strive to guarantee freedom of speech and movement, because of their desire for freedom and dignity for all. Aquarius-born are reputed to be cold and dismissive, but this is only their defense against premature touch. We need to learn how to embrace others and in a safe way to express their feelings.

Aquarius Friends and Family

Although the Aquarius-born are communicative, they need time to get closer to the people. Aquarius born are usually highly sensitive individuals, exposure to them implies risk. Their immediacy, combined with their clear points of view, allows them a threat. If required, Aquarius will do anything for a loved one to the point of self-sacrifice. Their friends should have the following three qualities: creativity, intellect and integrity. When it comes to the family, their expectations are nothing less than that. Although they have a sense of duty towards relatives, they will not have close ties if the same expectations as friendships are not fulfilled.

How to Entice the Aquarius Male

If you want to lure a man born under this zodiac sign, you will be acquainted with all of Aquarius' positive and negative aspects. Aquarius' people are erratic communicators, knowledgeable, emotional, confident and fantastic. Some of the negative characteristics of Aquarius include unreliability, stubbornness, indecision and inflexibility. If you want to seduce a man born under the sign of Aquarius astrology, you're going to have to be smart about it. If you ever come on too hard emotionally for this guy, he's never going to think about bringing you to bed.

The Aquarius guy will always exist within his own mind, and he wants a friend to speak about his radical thinking. So, if you're trying to seduce him, you can be buddies first. Many of their romances appear to begin as friendships that slowly grow into something more serious. This means Aquarius people never get into a romantic relationship with someone who's not already a mate. Respect the need for equality, your creativity, and the desire to make a difference in the world.

How to Attract the Aquarius Woman

Aquarius is an independent, mysterious, free-spirited and eccentric personality. Aquarius people have a unique sense of humor and a practical outlook on life. Nevertheless, confusion is a chronic problem for women raised under the Zodiac sign of Aquarius. The Aquarius woman longs for affection and a good conversation, though she may seem like a cold and distant human. She's a great sex buddy, but only if she's persuaded, you're involved in more than just a one night stand.

You will have to appeal to the many different sides of her personality if you want to seduce a wife born under the Aquarius Star. It's important to come across as a little different from everyone else she knows. The Aquarius woman is an extremely creative sex partner who wants to try different things on a regular basis. Yet make sure you let her know that she's more than just a sex partner to you.

The worst mistake you can make as you try to seduce the woman from Aquarius is to be greedy and pushy. Give her a lot of independence, because she's a really independent woman and she's not going to tolerate any kind of influence. Show her, in order to attract her attention, that you are the cool and calm type. The Aquarian woman does not like people who express their emotions publicly, thereby avoiding emotionally charged problems and attracting her intelligence instead.

Aries rules the head and leads the head, often literally walking the headfirst, leaning forward to speed and focus. His leaders are, of course, bold and seldom fearful of trial and danger. They are embodied youthful strength and energy, regardless of their age, and accomplish any assigned tasks rapidly.

ARIES FRIENDS AND FAMILY

The social life of the Aries leader is always going, pleasant and full of new interactions. We are tolerant of people we come into contact with, accepting of different personalities, and open-mindedness that can be caused by mere presence. Their circle of friends includes a wide range of odd personalities, mostly to make them feel like they have sufficiently different views about personal issues they don't know how to fix.

Because people born in the Aries sign easily enter into contact, straightforward and truthful in their approach, they can make an incredible number of connections and associates throughout their lifetimes. Yet, many of them have often been cut short for dishonesty and unclear motives. Long-term friendships in their lives will come with those who are just as energetic and brave enough to share their insides.

Family - Free and optimistic, Aries always decides where they want to go at a young age, splitting them from their families a little early. Even as infants, they can be difficult to control, and if they don't get enough love and patience from their parents, even their interpersonal relationships will fail later in life. A lot of anger arises from the sign of Aries, if there are too many constraints, and only when they come from radical families do, they fuel their bonds with a simple surge.

HOW TO ATTRACT THE ARIES MEN

This guy often considers the discovery of the target of his lust more enjoyable than the capture, and his winning disposition also lets him run for partners he can't have. To get his interest, one must play hard to get, as if to send out a message that he needs to fight for a reward, to attract the one that he always wants to be with. This is a man in love with a good challenge and in a hurry to become their partner's "Knight in Shining Armor," and he needs to be allowed to be one from time to time. His life partner might have to shout back in a battle, build strong barriers, and win his affection. Aries may be self-centered, arrogant, and stubborn on a bad day, but he is also brave, adventurous, and passionate.

Relationship with this man can be fun and exciting, but it's easy for someone to get hurt if their partner doesn't recognize the energy needed to last out their relationship.

HOW TO ATTRACT THE ARIES WOMAN

The women of Aries are fearless and natural leaders. They are energetic, charismatic, dynamic and in love with challenges and adventure. If you want to attract the attention of the Aries lady, you have to let her seduce you and cater to her independent nature. A woman born under the Zodiac sign of Aries is extremely passionate and erotic, rendering her attractive to the opposite sex. She is constantly on the move and will never enable herself to be overwhelmed by a man, finding love at the same time, while trying to hold onto power.

To attract a woman born in this symbol, one must take action, but not give the impression that authority has been taken away. She must be free to show initiative and fight for the affection of her loved one, expecting the same in return. When she falls in love, she becomes incredibly obedient and sometimes unnecessarily protective.

Dating means giving her all the attention she needs, giving her time and constant effort to prove that there is love behind the act. Confident and commanding, she doesn't just need someone to imitate, but someone to be similarly enthusiastic and powerful. Relationship with an Aries woman can be fascinating, full of adventure and anticipation, but only if one is willing to take on a less dominant role from time to time.

Compatible Signs Aries Should Consider: Sagittarius, Leo, Aquarius, Gemini, Libra CANCER ZODIAC SIGN

Element: Water Quality: Cardinal Color: White Day: Monday, Thursday

Ruler: Moon Greatest Overall Compatibility: Capricorn, Taurus

Lucky Numbers: 2, 3, 15, 20 Date range: June 21 - July 22

CANCER TRAITS

Strengths: Resourceful, highly inventive, supportive, compassionate, sympathetic, persuasive deficiencies: moody, negative, paranoid, cynical, dangerous

Cancer likes: Painting, residence-based hobbies, relaxation in or near the water, helping loved ones, a good meal with friends

Cancer dislikes: Strangers, any criticism of Mothers, revealing of personal life. Deeply emotional and nostalgic, cancer can be one of the most difficult zodiac signs to understand. We are very compassionate and sensitive, and we care deeply about the family and their house. Cancer is compassionate and connected to people close to them.

The sign of Cancer, like Scorpio and Pisces, belongs to the aspect of Air. Guided by passion and their spirit, they could have had a hard time fitting into the world around them. Being governed by the Sun, the phases of the lunar cycle intensify their internal complexities and establish transient emotional cycles beyond their grasp. As youngsters, they don't have enough coping and protective skills for the outer world, and they need to be treated with caution and compassion, because that's what they offer in exchange. Lack of empathy or even compassion shows itself through mood swings later in life, and even selfishness, self-pity, or coercion.

They're quick to help someone, just as they're quick to avoid conflict, and never profit from close combat of any kind, instead preferring to reach anyone harder, taller, or more effective than they expected. When in agreement with their life choices, Cancer members will be content and satisfied to be embraced by a loving family and love in their household.

CANCER FRIENDS AND FAMILY

When it comes to partnerships, Cancer members would happily interact with new social partners, but are highly sensitive to people who do not approve of their nearest surroundings. Filled with respect for the people who connect so effectively, they see all connections from their relational lens rather than simple curiosity or ranking. Most of all, they love socializing at home, where an enjoyable environment can be built, and deep knowledge can be exchanged under the conditions within their influence. Intuitive and caring, they can sometimes be interpreted from an incredibly rational point of view.

Family — Cancer is a sign of the soul; which people know more than any other sign of the zodiac about family bonds and their families. They tend to keep family memories intact for years to come with diligence and profound sentimentality. Once their personal lives are completed, they make wonderful, caring parents who seem to realize how children feel when they're miles away.

HOW TO ATTRACT THE CANCER MAN

A cancer man is cautious enough to realize that the effort is necessary, but he often fails to show it before he feels safe to do so. The friends need to make the first move, but still do it quietly to make him feel like he's leading the way. It is a complex individual, very emotional, reserved and excessively protective of his loved ones.

He wants the ideal wife and mother unintentionally because he loves women. He wants to feel needed and protective, to receive a lot of attention from his partner through kind words and subtle concerns and compliments to make his day. Although he may be moody, cynical, and clingy, he is an imaginative and supportive companion searching for someone to share a life with.

Cancer WOMAN can be quite difficult but deep inside, they're homely, conservative people. Their personality can be quite complicated. A woman with a Cancer sign is delicate, emotional, and unable to be comfortably in love. Once she has won her confidence, she will be loyal and faithful. To seduce her, one has to be careful to make the first move, acknowledging the need to be handled like a lady. She's not the right choice for someone hoping for a one-night stand, as she wants more from her mate than just casual encounters. Loving and ready to date, this woman needs a romantic partner who trusts in passion, but also is in touch with her unspeakable emotions.

Despite her careful nature, a Cancer woman is deeply erotic, and when she feels confident to show her true personality and emotions, she will express herself through an incredible sex life. To have a long-lasting relationship with a cancer woman, she needs someone who is faithful, respectful and honest, who does not forget betrayal and becomes very rigid and unpredictable when hurt. Compatible Signs Cancer Should Consider: Taurus, Virgo, Scorpio, Pisces,

Capricorn ZODIAC SIGN Element: Earth Quality: Cardinal Color: Brown, Black Day: Saturday Ruler: Saturn Greatest Overall Compatibility: Taurus, Cancer Lucky Numbers: 4, 8, 13, 22 Date range: December 22 - January 19

CAPRICORN TRAITS

Abilities: Responsible, focused, self-control, good managers Weaknesses: know-it - all, unyielding, snarky, assuming the worst Capricorn likes: family, tradition, music, understated status, high quality workmanship

Capricorn dislikes: Just about everything at a stage. Capricorn is a symbol of time and responsibility, and its signs are traditional and often very serious in nature.

Such people have an internal state of freedom that allows them to make significant progress in their personal and professional lives. They are practitioners of self-control, and they have the ability to lead the way, make sound and practical proposals and handle many of the people who work for them at all moment. They learn from their mistakes and get to the top, based solely on their experience and expertise.

Belonging to the element of Earth, such as Taurus and Virgo, this is the last sign in the trio of practicality and grounding. Not only do they concentrate on the material world, but they have the ability to make the most of it. Sadly, this aspect sometimes renders them rigid and sometimes too resistant to switch from one viewpoint or point of view to a partnership. We have a hard time accepting deviations from other individuals who are too far removed from their culture, and they may seek, out of insecurity, to actively enforce their traditional values.

The ruling planet of Capricorn is Saturn, and this planet represents all kinds of restrictions. The effect makes these people rational and responsible, but also hard, remote and unforgiving, vulnerable to feeling guilty and shifting to the past. They need to learn to forgive in order to make their own lives happier and more optimistic.

CAPRICORN FRIENDS AND FAMILY

Capricorn is wise, secure and trustworthy, and this renders its leaders faithful and extremely good mates, serving in one's life as foundations on the road to their dreams. We have to be surrounded by people who don't pose too many nosey questions, who know where the lines are, but who are dry, open-hearted and trustworthy enough to follow their lead. They're not going to gather too many mates in this period, but they're going to turn to those who make them feel at ease, wise and truthful at all times.

Family – This is a message with a full understanding of family traditions. Capricorns feel connected to every single thing from their history and adolescence, so they love to bring those memories out whenever the holiday season or the birthday season is close. This is an indication of a traditional disagreement over the supremacy of one's family, with their father and an extremely important individual in the manner that this person has developed his self-image over the years. As parents, they seem to be stern yet compassionate, able to take on the responsibilities that come with an infant.

HOW TO ATTRACT THE CAPRICORN MAN

Capricorn citizens are driven and competitive individuals who want to get to the top to get bonuses. He chooses truth to unattractive fantasies, but he is not afraid to set some of his more ambitious ideas in motion. His need for control is strong, and he might judge his partners, expecting them to be something they really aren't. His personality is twisted around success and obligation, and he often fails to put romantic relationships at the peak of his priority list.

The Capricorn guy wants to take care of himself and to be the one to make the rules from the beginning. He is searching for a realistic, balanced wife, and almost always ends up with an emotional one who has a hard time controlling his heart. When a relationship starts, he's going to think of how to honor the rule, but he's also going to show his feelings, wanting the person in front of him to feel comfortable and desirable sufficiently, no matter how much love he offers.

HOW TO ATTRACT THE CAPRICORN WOMAN

Capricorn people are creative, diligent, caring and trustworthy. She's always trying to find someone to make her happy, and she can't wait to reach up and feel the genuine tug of desire that lets her warmup with the possibilities that lay in the future. It would take her some time to lower her guard and also feel safe and comfortable enough to demonstrate how caring and open she can be when she's in love.

She expects her friends to be supportive, respectful so hard-working, and she needs to know that she's taken care of when something negative happens in the future. A Capricorn woman needs to feel comfortable with people she's meeting, so she requires time to decide what she expects from every relationship. Born in the Sun sign that Mars exalts, her intuition and determination are good, and this makes her a loving lover always in control of her own destiny, no matter what the circumstances.

Compatible Signs Capricorn Should Consider: Taurus, Virgo, Scorpio, Pisces TAURUS ZODIAC SIGN Colour: Red, Pink Day: Friday, Monday Ruler: Venus Best Overall Compatibility: Scorpio, Cancer Lucky Numbers: 2, 6, 9, 12, 24 Date range: April 20-May 20

TAURUS TRAITS

Abilities: Reliable, cautious, reasonable, committed, responsible, stable weaknesses: stubborn, clingy, uncompromising

Taurus likes: gardens, cooking, music, love, high-quality clothing, handwork

Taurus dislikes: abrupt shifts, problems, uncertainty whatsoever, synthetic fabrics Reasonable and well-founded., Taurus is the sign that the fruits of labor are harvested. We experience the need to be constantly surrounded by love and luxury, switched to the material world, hedonism, and physical pleasure. People born with the Sun in Taurus are sensual and responsive, finding touch and taste the most essential of all the senses.

This is one of the most stable and traditional signs of the zodiac, which is ready to stand and to decide before it reaches a degree of personal satisfaction. Taurus is a sign of the Moon, just like Virgo and Capricorn, and has the ability to see things from a rooted, rational and reasonable viewpoint. We find it easy to earn money and stay on the same tasks for years, even until they're done. What we often view as suffering can be seen as dedication, and it is amazing that they are capable of doing jobs. It makes them good mates, long-standing friends and partners, always there to love people. They may be overprotective, conservative, or materialistic, with world views based upon love of money and wealth. Earthly notes. The Taurus ruler is Venus, the world of love, beauty, gratitude, creativity and appreciation.

This gentle temperament will make Taurus a fantastic chef, a gardener, a lover and an artist. We are trustworthy and don't like sudden changes, disapproval or the feeling of shame that people are often susceptible to, being somewhat dependable on other people and feelings that they seem unwilling to let go of. Yet, no matter their potential emotional challenge, these individuals have the ability to bring a practical voice to reason in any chaotic and unsanitary situation.

TAURUS FRIENDS AND FAMILY

People born in this sign are trustworthy and always willing to lend a hand of friendship, though they can be closed to the outside world until they build trust in the new social connections they create. Many of their friendships begin in adolescence, with a propensity to last a lifetime. Once they make a clear intimate connection with another person, they will do whatever they can to nurture a relationship and make it work even in difficult times.

Family – Home and family concerns are of great importance to every Taurus. This is a person who loves children and appreciates the time spent with people who love them, who honor family traditions, rituals, and who are involved at all activities and gatherings.

They're going to enjoy throwing house parties with their family and friends, and don't mind cooking a meal for a room full of people if they're just having fun in exchange.

HOW TO ATTRACT THE TAURUS MAN

If you're searching for a solid, trustworthy and generous man, Taurus is the individual you're looking for. He is trustworthy, patient and tender when he is in love, always in search of a return of emotion. He's not going to pick up on the sly hinds and provocative looks of those who play with him, being a little slow on the uptake, as if waiting for someone to ask them out. He doesn't like any kind of artificiality, and loves discussions loaded with true statements, especially when it comes to congratulations and love declarations.

A Taurus takes time to build confidence, and anyone in search of his heart needs to take the time to earn it. As a human with very few words, often he appears difficult to reach, as if nothing would affect him. An invitation to a tasty home-cooked mean is always a safe bet when dating this guy, as well as choosing a spot that is relaxed and cozy rather than common or new.

Turned to instinct and conventional sense, sex is going to be seen as something that arrives when the time is right, he rarely puts some strain on his girlfriend, and acts like it's something to be appreciated, not something to be wanted. Part of his defined, stagnant nature is the apparent reluctance to forgive deception, so he needs to feel truly safe to stay with one companion for a long time.

HOW TO ATTRACT THE TAURUS WOMAN

If you want to seduce any woman born with her Sun in Taurus, you're going to have to appeal to her sense of romance. The ladies of Taurus want to be courted and eventually seduced, even when they have already agreed to enter into a relationship with someone. They like things to move gradually, and never fall into a romantic relationship easily and without thinking long and hard about their decisions. The woman of Taurus longs for true love and protection.

She has strong passion for lovely things and appreciates the beauty of good things in life, so the way to approach her is through enjoyable moments of interaction, respect for privacy, fine food and a gentle touch. This is a lady who doesn't like to feel rushed when she's dating and wants to take her time.

If at all she start to feel in any way comfortable and secure with someone else, It is very unlikely that she will quickly give in to her instincts and emotions, and if someone wants her trust, they will have to spend a lot of time and energy on the task of winning over her, making her feel comfortable. If she falls in love, she's affectionate, caring, polite and trustworthy, keeping to her partner for as long as she's faithful to her. She's going to give her heart freely and easily without holding back. Consistent Signs Taurus Must Consider: Jupiter, Virgo, Capricorn, Pisces

VIRGO ZODIAC SIGN Element: Earth Quality: Mutable Colour: Blue, Beige, Pale-Yellow Day: Wednesday Ruler: Mercury Best Overall Compatibility: Pisces, Cancer Lucky Numbers: 5, 14, 15, 23, 32 Date range: August 23 – September 22

VIRGO TRAITS

Strengths: Loving, logical, caring, hard-working, realistic weaknesses: shyness, insecurity, excessively critical of oneself and others, all work and no play

Virgo likes: Animals, healthy food, books, nature, and cleanliness

Virgo dislikes: Rudeness, seeking help, taking center stage Virgos often pay the smallest detail and attention with their deep sense of humanity often makes them the most attentive.

The methodical way of their life ensures that nothing is left to chance and while often tender, its heart can be shut to the outside world. This is a symptom and sign that is often overlooked, not because they lack the ability to articulate themselves, but because they do not recognize their emotions as real, accurate, or even important when they are contrary to any reason. The meaning behind the name speaks very well of their essence, born with the sense that, for the first time, they experience everything.

Virgo is a sign of the Moon that fits perfectly between Taurus and Capricorn. This will have a solid, but traditional, well-organized character and a great deal of practicality in their everyday lives.

Such people have an ordered existence, and even when they let go of uncertainty, their ambitions and aspirations still have tightly established lines of their heads. Constantly worried if they overlooked a fact that would be impossible to fix, they could get lost in the specifics, becoming overly critical and anxious with issues that nobody else seems to worry about.

VIRGO FRIENDS AND FAMILY

Virgos are excellent advisers, always knowing how to solve a problem. This can make them optimistic and extremely useful to get around, but it also shows their need to see the flaw with everything and everyone around them. They take care of the people with whom they build a solid friendship, respect them for years, and support them in every manner they can. I recognize culture and the value of duty, proud of their childhood, and all that rendered their minds as strong as they are.

HOW TO ATTRACT THE VIRGO MAN

One must fulfil his need for integrity and justice in order to seduce a Virgo man. In most cases, he cautiously, deliberately approaches dating and likes taking his time to meet someone before starting something dramatic. Once he receives information about what to expect from him, his wife must be sure to deliver nothing less. A Virgo guy may have a nice face, but don't let him trick you. He has intense and sensual desires, and only if his wife is patient enough to tolerate his propensity to over-analyze everything, can he finally warm up.

It takes apparent hard work to get a Virgo man out on his feet.

HOW TO ATTRACT THE VIRGO WOMAN

A Virgo's personality is a mixture of intelligence, attention to detail, common sense, and commitment, and a woman born with her in this sign is very smart, modest, and capable.

Trying to seduce this woman may seem daunting at first, because she is likely to be on the mask of indifference. Nonetheless, it is not cold but rational, reasonable and cautious when it comes to starting new relationships. She's never going to simply offer herself to someone without evaluating their nature and feelings that have been communicated with her since the beginning.

Under no conditions should she fall into the category of wealthy, materialistic women. As all the signs of the Sun, she should love the material world and see every present she earns as a blessing, but still enjoy things only when they are extremely practical and easy to use, handle, or when they need to be corrected.

Private and defensive, he's someone who needs the right partner to maintain his defense mechanisms but who is also vulnerable. Virgo Compatible Symptoms Should include: Taurus, Jupiter, Scorpio, Capricorn, Pisces

CHAPTER FOUR:

Nature And Significance Of Astrology

Nature of Astrology

A fascinating field of research investigated by several different experts is the association between perception in astrology and certain other characteristics of personality, although most such studies are conducted to prove that "believers" in star scientific method are in some way frail or deficient.

For instance, the Journal of Social Psychology published a piece by Ruth H. Sosis and others in February 1980 that discovered a fate theory strongly linked with such a belief in astrology. And in 1983, the same journal published a piece covering Michael Startup's study that found no signs of neurosis in students of astrology, although it found similarities between students of astrology and students of psychology.

Astrology varies from astronomy by focusing on the study of associations between astronomical events and events of human significance. Many people associate with only a small portion of star scientific knowledge, namely the Zodiac's twelve signs as they pertain to individual character and the use of astrology for divinatory purposes.

In the contemporary world, astrology holds a special position. The theory of the stars, however, tends to exercise control over the human brain, derided by many as medieval superstition. In addition, polls indicate that instead of faltering, its popularity is growing. The more entrenched we are now in the paradigm of "searching for one truth," explained in mathematical principles or physical laws, the more the significance of astrology is lost. Because this way of thinking has little to offer. Astrology embraces a completely different approach. Scientific thinking seems to be serving as censorship: it cannot be true what cannot be proven. It is not important to have subjective experience.

It is necessary to submit each event on Earth (and beyond) to some mathematical law. But when we interpret the universe through astrology, we realize that there is not a single truth or knowledge of events. Each of us gives our own truth for the moment and place of birth. One of today's world's expectations is that scientific reality is the path to a better and more sustainable future.

Evidence is taken of predictive statements and the ability to control powerful and dangerous forces. We are now flying aircraft, taking pictures of the strong chaotic powers of the beginning of our Universe, can calculate the amount of radiation and can stop many diseases in many cases.

Astrology has been, and still is, closely linked to the occult, and there have never been any physical "vibrations" or factors that influence to account for all the astrological effects. Moreover, most people who were attracted to astrology were also naturally attracted to the occult. These had the purpose of providing a "political" view of the world to those who were drawn to science but considered the various secular ideologies, such as moral humanism, personally cold and unsatisfactory. In order to obtain this amount of knowledge, objectivity and distancing oneself from the object of analysis were shown as crucial. Astrology has little to offer in this paradigm.

Yes, it is possible there have been many attempts to prove astrology scientifically but, honestly speaking the civilized world has been home to a loud minority of self-appointed defenders of human reason, since at least the historical era known as the Enlightenment, who railed against religion or anything close that dared suggest that the human being was nothing more than a physiological-chemical entity.

Despite the antagonism of militant fundamentalists and conservative republicans, astrology has steadily grown over the past centuries. This growth may well be related to the declining authority of the critics of astrology. Astrology's interpretation as a paradox may give human lives more meaning. Dark and angry. Indeed, I believe that one of humanity's defining marks is its constant exposure to paradoxes.

For instance, the tension between the heavens and the Earth's dust fills us with the encouraging spirit of excellence and justice yet enslaving us to a worldly nature that demands addressing our physical needs. Much has been said against astrology, published and debated. Physicists would strongly argue that stars are far from us and that the force that keeps the Sun and planets together cannot affect human beings— objects of negligible mass compared to planets.

Besides the four fundamental powers- electromagnetic, solid, electromagnetic and gravitational–will any other force that these massive rotating masses would inflict on masses of our dimensions be treated as preposterous by physicists without any reservations? It is true in most cases, people who have not researched astrology in depth are carrying out the rant against astrology.

Astrology was grouped together with everything else that didn't fall within a rather limited scientific definition into the bracket of unjustified superstition. Why however, is astrology irrational?

When you live near a seaside and are sensitive to the cyclical nature of the ocean, you can clearly see that the Sun and the Moon regulate the tides. How big a step is it to affirm that human beings are influenced by celestial bodies? We cannot touch, taste, or see the powers of astrology, but we cannot touch, taste, or see gravity either. In terms of its influence, gravity is experienced only indirectly. In this way, astrologers may respond, they perceive astrological powers adversely, in regard to human influence and other global events.

In addition, as astrologers may argue, the techniques of objective, quantitative analysis can be applied to astrological statements, as was done most significantly in Michel and Françoise Gauquelin's work. In the strict sense, therefore, astrology is not illogical. An interesting observation is that some remarkable parallels can be observed in a significant number of parents and their children's horoscopes.

Many planets, not specifically Jupiter and Saturn (which take 11,8613 and 29,4568 years to complete one revolution round the sun and can therefore easily justify repeatability), are in parent's horoscopes either in similar situations or in similar ratios. To step forward in an attempt to understand the appeal of astrology for the typical citizen of an industrialized society, it must be remembered that even for those people with a small degree of confidence in mainstream religion, normal, everyday life — the universe as it is lived on a daily basis — appears to be meaningless. Astrology breaks with the concept of a single verifiable truth, demonstrated by objective, unbiased scrutiny.

It can, therefore, empower us: it reminds us that while fateful to a natal chart, we are a process that is unfolding, possibly without any goal whatsoever. We're not one but many, we're only a constant being, a constant being. Astrology, he presented a scientific hypothesis relating to human beings' celestial influences. He suggested that due to all the differing gravitational influence of planets on both the Sun's magnetic field, the magnetic disturbances produced in the Sun, each of which is unique to different planets, cause changes in the Solar Wind, which continually affects the fetus when it enters the Earth. The effect of each planet in accordance with the already articulated (formed) genetic traits that affect the birth of the child and the development of the child.

He also categorically defined that in shaping human beings, each individual planet will play a selective role. His key scientific explanation is that Sun magnifies the planets ' gravitational effects in the form of global magnetic fields. This concerns human beings. Until now, it is challenging to condemn this interpretation until stalwart opponents of astrology. Every planet is accountable for some characteristics in astrology.

In addition, two different space points (Rahu and Ketu) mark the two overlapping points in the Earth's orbit around the sun (Ecliptic) to the Moon's orbital plane. So much so that they are regarded as two planets are also considered necessary. The importance of these two concepts is well known to a student of astrology in predicting such important factors such as success, disasters, defeats, survival, etc.

Once, planets in astrology have different meanings between Rahu-Ketu axis and planets between Ketu-Rahu axes. Many citizens feel at the hands of social, cultural, and political powers that they barely recognize, much less anticipate. Though outsider astrology seems unattractive due to its obvious determinism, it helps people to understand the issues in their lives as part of a real, predictive mechanism in which they can gain some influence.

Theories of Astrological Influence Strategies to clarify how astrology "works" shift between two poles, one that emphasizes the study of stars as a natural science (and therefore seeks to distinguish them from occultism), and the other which, while often called astrology by the interest of science, stresses the metaphysical or mystic aspect of the study of terrestrial factors.

If astrology is not scientific, why would two space points, and even that, attached to the Earth's orbital plane, assume so much importance? Astrology communicates with each entity as a dimensional being, defining all the individual's characteristics. It speaks of personality, health, affluence, intellectual ability, relationships, and family.

While all of these aspects are clearly obvious, others are intangible and concealed, involving potentials such as chance, ability to gain wealth, ability to acquire skills, and all the other biological aspects associated with the person such as mother, father, brother, sisters, relations, wife, children, etc. So, here is an environment where a person is defined by his / her multi-dimensional character. It is now clearly established that individual traits are attributable to their genes.

The observable traits such as personality, voice, intelligence and illnesses are linked to the genes, to name a few. Another strong indication that planetary factors play a crucial role in influencing genetic mannerisms in individuals is that planetary variations can also characterize them.

Expression of gene mutations that result in certain features and suppression of few genes that may arise at a later stage in life also shows that planetary transition should regulate them. The genetic factor is the one that brings out the similarities between different parents at the very same location, including that of the twins, between individuals born at the same time.

The variations in the level of expression will depend on the circumstances genetic make-up that causes for a difference in degree rather than the form. Unified Field Theory and its related String (and newly Brane) Theory are still debating on a universe of 10-32 dimensions (or more) with four dimensions of space and time and the additional possible unknown dimensions.

Astrology clearly outlines the universe's multi-dimensional features. So, on the one side, astrology connects huge masses like planets and human beings characterized by DNA molecular strands of genes. It thus reflects the convergence of all four fundamental forces (electromagnetic, strong, weak, and gravity), while Science is unable to even combine all these four fundamental forces, gravity disregarding convergence, while the other three forces— solid, heavy, and electromagnetic — integrate. Nothing too small, in spite of these planets' masses and travel times from the Earth.

Nevertheless, gravity varies with weight and size. The consequences of Planetary Retrogression are yet another area worth mentioning in which the apparent regressive motions of the planets caused by the planets' relative motions with reverence to that of the Earth clearly demonstrate that these planets' motions have a marked scientific implication. About the dates of Saturn and Jupiter in particular, retrogression and de-retrogression (resumption of forward motion), anybody can witness the occurrence of definitive issues that had been lingering without end for a certain time before.

The distance between the corresponding planet and the Moon in Retrogression is the shortest. If there were such a scientific basis in astrology, why should distance play a role? Don't let us forget that some of these time-tested discoveries were made long before Johannes Kepler formulated the Laws of Planetary Motions and Sir Isaac Newton's Law of Gravity, brilliant astrological minds.

Astrology concerns with the possibility of occurrence of dimensions in humans–the existence, magnitude and time of such manifestations being determined by planetary locations and their co-ordinate motions. There are a few misunderstandings like the nodes of Sun, Moon and Moon as planets and Earth as the nucleus that can be resolved through combined efforts. So, too.

Periodic observances such as Rahu Kala and Yamagantaka have no meaning in a continuously varying function such as time. While the current empirical correlations suggest quite a number of general principles, a connection between' One Cause One Result' is still missing in astrology.

Astrology: Is it Scientific? Astrology can seem scientific in some ways. This uses scientific knowledge about celestial bodies and scientific sounding devices, such as star charts. Many people use astrology to create perceptions about future events and the personalities of people, much as expectations are generated by scientific ideas.

And some argue that evidence supports astrology — people's experiences that feel astrology has worked for them. Even with these science trappings, is astrology really a way of answering questions scientifically? Here we will use the Science Checklist to determine one way astrology is widely used. See if you think that would count as science! Concentrate on the natural world?

The basic premise of astrology is that heavenly bodies— the sun, moon, planets, and constellations — have control over earthly events, or are associated. Does the natural world want to be explained? Astrology uses a set of rules concerning the relative positions and movements of celestial bodies to produce forecasts and explanations for events on Earth and characteristics of human personality.

For instance, a child born just after the spring equinox is likely to become an entrepreneur in some forms of astrology. Use tried and tested ideas? Several expectations generated by astrology are so general that every outcome can be interpreted as trying to fit the expectations; if treated that way, astrology is not testable. Others, however, have employed astrology to produce very specific expectations that could be tested against natural world outcomes.

For instance, one's Zodiac sign impacts one's ability to command respect and authority according to astrology. Since these characteristics are important in politics, we might predict that if astrology really clarified the personalities of the people, scientists will be more likely to have Zodiac signs identified by astrologers as "favorable" to science.

The astrological theories are testable if used to create specific expectations like this one.

Are you building on evidence?

The evidence does not back up the validity of astrological theories in the few instances where astrology was used to produce testable expectations and the findings were tested in a detailed study. This experience is typical in science— scientists frequently check ideas that turn out to be wrong. One of science's hallmarks, however, is that ideas are adjusted when the evidence warrants them. In response to contradictory evidence, astrology didn't change its ideas, Does the scientific community get involved? Having shared one's findings and critically assessing others ' outcomes are not integral parts of astrology practice.

An astrologer may go all his or her career without presenting findings at a scientific meeting or publishing a single article. When astrologers publish these articles are normally not peer-reviewed or published in places where the scientific community will critically scrutinize them.

Misconception in Astrology

Astrology is traditional, nearly as old as when the first time was measured by man. It is and has always been present in all countries and cultures in some form. In reality, most of the population of the world is using astrology on a daily level and not only for entertainment, as we are doing the West here.

It may be necessary to brush away some popular misconceptions about astrology before we start our study of astrology. One popular misconception regarding astrology is that the planets in the heavens are causing events to occur here on Earth. Professional astrologers I have known, and I have known many of them, do not hold onto these ideas of "celestial influence"— theories that perhaps the planets somehow make something happen to us; instead, modern astrologers see the heavens and the Earth as whole, interpenetrating and occupying the same space and time that is actually the case. The columns of the horoscope are abstract and available to all. Interestingly, I couldn't agree more! But let's take a closer look at why this might be the case before we throw the baby out with the bath water.

Who's really going to say we're all so different from each other to start with? It could reasonably be assumed that when we look from a wider evolutionary perspective, we are probably more similar to each other than we are distinct. Human beings end up sharing the same DNA as any other living person 99.9 percent. We are all consuming, drinking, sleeping, dreaming, finding equilibrium and affection, coping badly at times, desiring material possessions or exciting experiences, becoming overly sensitive and anything else. As for the whole matter of astrology, columns of horoscopes are merely the iceberg's very tip.

Did you know you were supposed to read the columns of the horoscope for both your Sun and the rising sign? Indeed, if you have access to your natal chart, you can read all 12 of the horoscopes as they affect you personally. Many other sceptics of the credibility of the horoscope column often denounce these mildly designed claims by suggesting that astrologers engage in the 'Barnum Effect.'

The Barnum Effect suggests that the recipient will forcibly identify with the assumptions based on their signs by stating publicly vague and related statements about personality. Science is an analytical research method. What does it mean? It implies that science tries to answer objective questions with such a materialistic filtration system of the world by observing natural phenomenon. Science requires the senses to extract data that can be assembled into a law or theory.

Biology, physiology, geomorphology, physics, chemistry, astronomy, zoology and many more are included in a list of general sciences. Though it has been argued that areas such as psychology, philosophy, sociology, and other fields of human behaviour are not recognized as scientific disciplines directly. Why is it?

There is a serious shortage of scientific data to study. What's in common with all feelings, opinions, sensitivity, temperament, morality and ethics? These are results of a process that is not materialistic. Consciousness is among the most overlooked fields of study within the sciences, and yet it's something that is enmeshed with every one of us. By social studies, such as humanities, these interactions are usually sorted out.

In fact, astrologers are observing society behaviours and associating the practice with the stars. Inherently, astrology makes no factual statements about the planets or their effects on human behaviour. Astrology does not include supernatural beliefs, psychic powers, mystical activity, and sorcery. To put it simply, astrology is a method used to study human nature and the environment.

Modern day 'psychics' and paranormal forms appear instead of the other way around to project their beliefs into the research. There really is no system of beliefs needed to study astrology. Nonetheless, I strongly suggest that after reading your chart and understanding such placements around your 3rd, 8th, 9th, and 12th houses. An astrologer manages to see astrology in a manner similar to a weather forecast being seen by a meteorologist.

The stars never compel anyone to act in a particular way but indicate the types of energetic patterns that may arise. With all this in mind, the amount of forms that astrology is realistic is extreme, almost unfathomable. I will keep this misunderstanding short by listing only a few simple ways in which I use astrology personally:

To understand better my personality (read my birth chart and take a careful look at how I act) To understand better the personality traits of other people (e.g. friends, relatives, famous people, scholars, political leaders). To aid in planning my future wisely, Transits, harmony, synastry (Studying how and where planets and many others are influencing my energy; mood changes, extension / opportunity, shadow elements, etc.)

To understand better psychology, philosophy, sociology, culture, cycles, and background. To realize how my time and effort can be optimized (Horoscopes) Scheming insight yields over long periods of time (Solar arrives, Jupiter returns, Saturn returns, etc.) The list continues on and on... life is a painting canvas. How helpful would it be to know which kind of themes will prevail over the coming months or years in your life? Can you make rational choices differently?

Astrologers are uneducated scientifically, superstitious, or do not understand the modern psychology, etc. You may be surprised in learning, that mere studying astrology is not an easy thing. It turns out it is very difficult to research the relative position of the stars regularly or even to understand the enormity of the whole topic.

Astrology has been a subject for the intellectual elite of the ages throughout history. There was astrology prior to astronomy. There was astrology also prior to modern medicine. Today, this tradition is continuing. Most astrologers today are very well trained, some with PhDs and master's degrees in astrology. Astrologers are just con artists who aim to extract money from gullible victims.

The first aspect to be addressed is this unpleasant notion of the exchange between the recipient ("victim") and the reader ("con-artist"). Envision a scenario in which a person thinks he will see an authentic astrologer. The astrologer will look at the overall structure of the recipient's natal chart to identify the stars, signs, house location, dominant elements, and placement aspects.

The astrologer will then talk about just how he / she thinks all work together to create an overall personality through the placements' influence. It is worthy and valuable to have different kinds of perceptions. In fact, each astral map is like a further and further into rabbit hole, searching for new meanings. A chart's interpretation is never shut but is always open.

Significance of Astrology

Astrology enables us to integrate our existences into cycles that are greater. It teaches us to be respectful, that our time on this earth is nothing compared to eternity of the Universe, and that other things are equally (or maybe more) significant. It's a way to talk to the supernatural as well. "One values the Earth since it is one's mother, an animal because it can be a resurrected ancestor, and the stars because they become messengers, guardians and custodians."

"Astrology is a script," as Dane Rudhyar puts it "The vocabulary of astrology." The only thing necessary is to comprehend the language. In reality, it appears that the moment of astrology is of great importance because it opens a dialog with all the above to reach an agreement about our destiny.

In addition, humanistic and psychological moves closer to astrology promote one (or both) the belief that there is a purpose in our creation (as depicted in the planetary cycles)–a destiny to achieve that goes over and above our ego's limits–or that the astral chart can be a wonderful tool for social-awareness and self-knowledge. Such claims can be used to reinforce astrology's value.

They are colored in accordance with our current societal values, however: development, goal-centered aspirations, functionality, and practicality. If it's useful, astrology is essential. Yes, our art tells us that the question of meaning is linked to the question of action. For the 2nd house of principles is training the 6th house of routine and useful things in the astrological houses system.

It's only rational that most roles should strive to make it beneficial in order to make astrology relevant. Indeed, some sort of religious narcissism has made people believe that our offenses and sufferings are intended to help us grow into a better self. According to this idea, people hope to gain enlightenment as if it were a matter of career: by maintaining such steps dictated by some religious authority that would ensure grace and wisdom.

But this is a misconception of the word evolution (as evolution occurs without any intent or intention). Therefore, attachment–even if it is to a religious doctrine –would possibly impede the attainment of higher consciousness. One of today's world's assumptions is that scientific truth is the way to a fuller and more real future. Proof is taken of statistical claims and the ability to control powerful and dangerous powers. We are now flying aircraft, taking pictures of the powerful chaotic forces of the beginning of our Universe, can determine the amount of radiation and can avoid many diseases in many cases. Astrology has little to say in this model.

Yes, it is true there have been several attempts to prove astrology scientifically but, frankly, most of them end up failing. Dennis Elwellv explains how difficult it can be to prove astrology scientifically as "the cosmos might have its own categories" and not those we use to assess astrological manifestations (including many other reasons). On the stand of divination, Geoffrey Corneliusvi appears to suggest that the validity of a chart interpretation depends on whether it matters to somebody or not. Astrology is an ancient practice that says that at the moment of birth, human character and fate depend on the location of the stars.

Nevertheless, we also believe that in order to improve the quality of life, astrology requires concrete and realistic adjustments of each person. Astrology advocates free will life and opposes fatalism and superstition. This also allows us to understand our character more critically, to acknowledge our strengths and abilities, and an incentive for emotional and spiritual maturation.

It is important to underline here that in Greece the deductive analysis was founded as the reaction to the compelling speech of the orators, sophists and politicians of that period. Although in a particular period of history it was formed as a solution to societal desires, it eventually became essentially the reality method.

The more reinforced we are now in the paradigm of "searching for one truth," explained in mathematical formulae or physical laws, the more important astrology loses. For this has nothing to offer to a certain mode of thought. Astrology embraces a completely different approach. Scientific thinking seems to be acting as censorship: it cannot be true what cannot be proved. It is not necessary to have subjective experience.

Various perceptions are equally deserving and valuable. For example, we know that Jupiter can be positioned in different signs and houses or in different planetary aspects in each chart, which means that many different ideologies are equally credible and valuable. The same applies to the rest of the astrological factors. It is important to apply every occurrence on Earth (and even beyond) to some mathematical law.

Yet when we interpret the universe through astrology, we realize there is not a single truth or knowledge of events. This gives every one of us our own reality for the moment and place of birth. Astrology helps us analyze our history, present and future choices–generating insights that allow us to examine our unconscious choices. It certainly helps us to be more compassionate about ourselves, our past 'mistakes' and our tendency to fight when we didn't know better! We're doing better because we know better! When we become more alert and higher in consciousness, this means that life becomes simpler. Astrology will help us to better understand our past events.

Astrology also helps in relaxing and enjoying health, prosperity and spiritual advancement as well as helping to avoid strains in marital relationships, business and professional matters. Using astrology, we will figure out what attributes we are looking for in a partner and how to solve any conflict, as we will have a greater understanding of different personalities. Some agree that astrology is a gift to mankind because it has many advantages. Check out which astrology's 3 greatest benefits:

Better Knowledge of Different Individuals: Horoscope can provide us with an insight into the mentality and behaviours of the individuals we interact with. It allows us to better adjust to each other's weaknesses and strengths, and we can also avoid conflicts and minimize the negative effects of character differences.

A View into the Future: Astrology is a sacred science that helps us to look forward to the future. Astrology will explain what we expect to happen, what forces are ahead of us, and when is the right time to step up to achieve your goals. In this way we can make the decisions easier if we have at least a basic idea of what awaits us.

Compatibility of relationships: Many people seem to believe that studying our astrological chart will inform us with which signs we are compatible. The contrast between two astrological charts will decide the relationship of the two individuals, whether they include intimacy, business relations or friendships. Casting horoscopes involve name, date, conception and time of birth are triggered by astrological evidence.

Astrologers base their research on this data as they analyse planet patterns and positions as they rise, ultimately end, and set the signs. The quality of their results depends whether they perform a research study or personal horoscope, whether or not their data is accurate. They cannot justify their work unless they can validate their data, whether they present a paper or delineate a map.

Speculative charts come from cases in which the time of birth is unknown and as such are pure speculation, usually backed up by events to show the supposed accuracy; chart rectification begins with an approximate time of birth and adjusts the chart to a specific minute. Historically, no source of origin has been identified with astrological results. Magazines and newspapers blithely display charts and documents, and readers generally acknowledge the accuracy of the data.

Astrologers are giving lectures or delivering articles with no data source. If you start looking at the charts of historical figures and public figures, it may come as a surprise to see that birth is given many times. There are more than a hundred birthdates for Ronald Reagan, Joseph Stalin, Clark Gable and Evita Peron. Nothing is wrong with theoretical evidence — seeing it as that.

Nevertheless, it is a mistake to present data as true when it is not: Deliberate inaccuracy is morally inexcusable; and it is novice, disrespectful, and dishonest to present data without a source. Many astrological data are moment-specific, so any chart which does not state the source is subject to debate and any conclusions reached from such a chart as valid conclusions are not acceptable. Astrologers take what they can get when data was scarce.

This time is gone should they ever seek to gain a reputation for carrying out legitimate studies.

CHAPTER FIVE:

Horoscope

What is a Horoscope?

The actual term ' horoscope' comes from the Latin combination of two words in which' Horo' means hour and' Scope' means view, so it is a' vision of the hour.' Another meaning of' horoscope' is that this is a delineation of different celestial forces focused on celestial patterns as seen in publications or newspapers. As astrologers we lay claim to the horoscope as a person's astrological chart or a particular time estimated from planetary positions either in the orbital period or tropical zodiac. The equations used are centered on birthdate, location and time.

This is why a horoscope, like a fingerprint, is so unique. When an astrologer continues to work with a timely chart, the energies it carries are unique to that individual. Be aware that the planets ' chart energies and signs serve as the individual's potential for artistic expression. The horoscope continues to hold planets, signs, aspects, houses, and other points within it that reflect potential features and patterns.

It is our natural will that enables us to be articulated in other ways to work with these trends or remould them. Most people seem to think our fate is written in stone by the horoscope. Not quite so! It looks promising by the way, but our personal prerogative is how we use these potentials. What the horoscope is able to offer is insight and awareness of these potentialities and their uses.

The Houses

We've all seen an astrological chart wheel divided into twelve pie-shaped, roughly equivalent sections, as much as we'd cut an apple pie or pizza. These twelve sections are termed "Astrological Houses," or usually just "The Houses." One or more of the planets, or the Sun, or the Moon, may be found in each pie-shaped house. Just as somebody could tell you that they have the Sun in Aries, so they could also say they have the Sun in the 11th house.

Such twelve quarters, like the Zodiac's twelve signs, have specific meanings. Coincidentally, a house in astrology is like a clock. The zodiac is divided into twelve different divisions or buildings, each of which is regulated by another star. The term "He's a Taurus" could just as easily be "He's a Second House Sun." We'll know more about what the houses say, but first, knowing more about what they are and where they come from will be beneficial.

What houses are there?

Houses are first of all part of your horoscope, part of your birth chart. The houses are simply a way of dividing the space around your birthplace into sections: the space above a certain place, the space below, the space to the east, to the west... and so on. We divide the whole space into twelve sections, just as there are orange segments.

Once we have divided the room, we look to see that in which section (house) the various celestial bodies can also be found, like where the Sun and the Moon are. Where are the planets, and where are the stars, or any other astronomical bodies of interest to us? And as the planets are plotted in the signs of the zodiac, most house systems show in which each house begins and ends with the Zodiac band.

Houses are Three Dimensional, although we have a two-dimensional (flat) horoscope map, the houses parts are not. They are three-dimensional as are the colored sections. Imagine going outside under the evening sky, with the planets and stars glowing all over you, and afterwards imagine trying to divide all that space, the space above and below you (on the other side of the earth) into twelve sections or segments. From where you stand, looking south, there would be the tenth house, behind you and north (and below you) there would be the fourth house, the first house on your left and east, the seventh house on your right and west and so on, and so on. This is what houses in astrology are.

House Cusps

House cusps are ascertained by taking the 3-dimensional sections of the house (remember the coloured segments) and seeing how those lines intersect and cross the Zodiac.

The cusp for each house is where these lines cross the Zodiac and the Zodiac sign is the "sign for the house cusp." You can see the segments of the house in the chart above, and you can also see the ring of the twelve signs of the Zodiac. A cusp is the imaginary line in astrology that divides a pair of consecutive signs in the zodiac or horoscope quarters. The houses are segments of the ecliptic plane at the time and place of the respective horoscope (a wide circle representing the Sun's orbit as seen from the Earth). We are classified counter-clockwise from the cusp of the first house. Houses one to six are usually below the horizon and houses seven to twelve are above the horizon, but some systems might not completely respect the division (especially if the ascendant disagrees with the first house's cusp).

The various methods of calculating house divisions stem from disagreement as to what they mean mathematically (in terms of time and space). In Western astrology, all house systems use twelve houses projected on the ecliptic. The differences arise from whatever basic plane is the object of the initial division or whether the divisions represent time units or distance degrees if space is really the basis for the division of the building, the selected plane will be split into arcs of 30 ° C.

It is before the eclimactic is projected whether these divisions are made straight on, or on the celestial equator, or on some other great circle. When time is at the base of the division of the room, the disparity between the households' invariance of the same time (each house is 2 hours per day of visible sunlight), or the hour of the day (day and night are split into six sections, but the spatial period differs according to the season or latitude).

In spite of these different approaches, all house divisions in Western astrology have several similarities: the twelve cusps of the house are always projected onto the ecliptic; they always position the cusp of the first house near the eastern horizon and each cusp of the house is 180° longitude apart from the sixth house (1st opposes 7th; 2nd opposes 8th and so forth). Since the solar disk is about half a degree in diameter, the Sun will straddle the cusp as it travels across the sky.

Where each section crosses the Zodiac, band is where there is a sign on a cusp of the room. Even though most house systems are divided into the acquainted twelve houses, there are several different types of house systems; that is, there are many various ways to divide the space around us.

The ecliptic is also subdivided into twelve parts of 30 degrees in the equal house system, although the houses are quantified in increments of 30 degrees starting from the ascendant degree. It starts with the ascendant, which serves as the 'cusp' or point of departure of the 1st house, then the 2nd house starts exactly 30 degrees later in zodiac order, then the 3rd house starts exactly 30 degrees later in Zodiac order from the 2nd house, etc. Astrologers always want to argue between themselves as to which house system is really the best, and agree to differ on just this Trying to explain the differences between house systems is far too complicated to jump into here, so it will have to be enough to know that although there are different house systems, these systems tend to agree on the main points, and therefore they are more the same than different.

Using any of the major systems, you should feel confident; at least until you are experienced enough to argue over each other's merits. So much to give you an amazing image of what houses are, WHY they are critical is of greater concern. What are they going to mean? / Why Houses Are Important.

If we can assume that the planets tell everyone what general area of life we are dealing with and that whichever sign of the Zodiac a particular planet or planets is in tells us something about the energy process of that area of life, then we could conclude that the houses tell us where all of this activity is happening. Let's make a simple example: I happen to be in the 8th house with the Sun in Cancer. What does it mean? Let's take a look at this. The Sun seems to be the self, the self to which each of us seeks, the self to which we expect (and can even) become — what we look up as our future.

The Zodiac sign Cancer states that this Sun (self) can be very sensitive, that we (of this sign) are far down there, and also that we feel and imagine things very much. We also know that perhaps the sun signs of Cancer love their homes. And finally, the 8th house (criticism) is the assessment house, which breaks down things, picks up kernels and throws the chaff away — it's all about it.

The eighth house is also the secret and enigmatic house of study. Am I one of those things? I do. I've often worked at home; even though I had a company with 650 employees, I stayed at home as much as I could humanly. Also, for sensitivity, some other things may have to be added to my wife, but for many years I was sensitive enough to make my living as a musician. Okay, this is where I shine when I'm a critic.

I created and built the All-Music Guide (as well as other entertainment guides) and today the All-Music Guide is the biggest music criticism collection on the planet. I love mystical and occult topics and have researched them throughout my life; indeed, throughout this course, I intend to highlight some mysterious astrological concepts. This (above) is just one representation; of course, there are several, many ways to interpret "the 8th House Sun in Cancer" and that's what makes astrology so fascinating, once you are in touch with your own inner power. An oracle is something we speak to or through us. Knowing what's going on is more interesting than trying to talk about astrology in keeping with our own personal beliefs. The astrological houses describe the horoscope's exact areas of life.

Home, for example, represents something entirely unique; it defines the different types of people, locations, and circumstances of life that you experience in this lifetime.

The Twelve Houses Description

Each one of the twelve houses have a different meaning, each explaining or pointing out a different area of our life. When we know more about what each of these areas of knowledge means, we can start reading astrological phrases such as the one mentioned above, "Sun in Cancer in the Eighth House." And, best of all, the wheel of the twelve houses itself is a single, full process (like the zodiac signs, the Moon phases, etc.).

So that every house in the process is a step, one leading to the next; thus, when you learn about cycles and cycles, you learn about the houses automatically.

First House

The First House is about you, who you are, and how you appear or come across to others— the influence you are having on your first meeting. It's the total sum of what you've managed to get together in your life so far and what you can bring on the table for everyone to see— your complete package. There is usually tremendous restlessness reinforced by easy-going demeanour, but travel love is likely to be heavily marked. There is no doubt that a roving existence is highly improbable.

Sociability appears to be a strong feature, and in all those occupations there is likely to be considerable ability that puts the person in constant contact with the general public. The horoscope's first house is the sign of the zodiac you'd see on the eastern horizon at the time the figure is made for. Much depends on the factors that can be created in the ascendant planets and other planets. The first house is the house that controls your physical appearance, the picture that you project, and the first impact you make on others. Here, the Zodiac archetype's energy also explains how something new begins. This is comparable to your defence mechanisms and relation with new environments, as it is an ego and surface self-mechanism. The native will have an excellent mind if the aspects are good and can rise high in the world.

The attitude is going to be good that he or she is going to have many mates, even though bad planets are in the ascendant but are well expected. If evil appearances are formed, the native is fickle, able to change, unstable, often quickly tempered and misleading. It governs the native's personal appearance, and to some extent influences the mind, especially if there is any planet in the ascendant. The world is called the co-ruler in the ascendant. If the ascendant is an evil galaxy-Saturn, Mars, or Uranus, the native would have on the head a spot, mark, or scar.

Second House

The Second House have to do with material possessions, but also with how you acquire, measure, and love things in life. It marks your potential (or lack of it) to build on what you have been given and to incorporate your plans and ideas towards something significant and durable. Your values come in here. This is the money and material possessions house.

It covers your finances, personal belongings, and your physical and spiritual connection to the gifts you have. How are your ways of spending? This chart area belongs to the Venus-ruled Taurus, and its key phrase is "I have."

In this section of the chart, your self-worth and self-esteem always come alive. Thrift will play a major role in the accumulation Financial variations are likely to be significant, but they appear to be satisfactory. The main danger seems to lie in a pronounced love of affluence and extravagance in general. Nevertheless, spasmodic spells of great thrift and commitment to simple life counterweight these traits.

Third House

The Third house is all about connecting and interacting, how to reach out, discover, and generally communicate with both people and things— your ability to connect.

All forms of correspondence are conveyed, whether written or spoken, by telephone or e-mail, confidential or in public. The third house controls the method of thought, communication style, and cognitive functioning. As well as your immediate surroundings, it determines the energy of your general exchanges. It includes the brothers and sisters, cousins, friends and early education.

Love for change and variety is probable to stimulate travel and interest in such occupations as newspaper work, where novelty is the prevalent element. Publicity can be very sexy. Mental activity, potentially at the price of superficiality, expands the range of interests. Assimilative ability makes people easily trained, but the driving force tends to come from creativity instead of intelligence.

Fourth House

Family life tends to become an important element in personality development, and the main interest is usually focused on domestic issues. Frequent terminations tend to happen but gains from houses and land are typically expected. Financial benefit can also be derived from heritage. It is about the overall lifestyle experience you draw around you and how you feel about life, particularly when it comes to home and family issues — your specific safety cover.

The House of Home is commonly called the Fourth House. We put in mind that place where we put down our roots when we think about home. We are setting our foundation and, as it were, planting ourselves squarely on Earth. One day, we're going to return to the same planet. The Fourth House draws the whole circle of things by also addressing old age, endings and our final place of rest. We make ourselves a home, or more precisely for ourselves, by laying down roots.

It's important to note we've really brought home the essential self in addition to the outside home (all the bricks and mortar around us). 'home.' They have a peaceful ring for the words themselves. The self is now mainly focused, immersed, one with the Earth in peace. We try to come home for ourselves and for those we love, physically and psychologically. By creating a home, we develop a meeting place for ourselves and others, a safe haven, a sacred place. We incorporate the self with everything that has come before us in our home and has helped shape what we have been today. We are creating a domestic space that will soothe and nurture us and keep those we love safe. Family history, cultural and social norms and ways of being are also important here.

All these, like our ancestry, roots and heritage, are governed by the Fourth House. Through us, these qualities are brought' home' to the place we call home. However, much of the Fourth House's emphasis is on the home concept. Your Inner Foundation Within you, the fourth house rules the home and the one in which you grew up. This chart field, governed by Mother Moon, can decide your origins, your sense of safety, and your emotional basis.

This house is also about your past relation with your line of ancestors. None other than responsive Cancer belongs to this lunar influence; its key phrase is "I feel." The Fourth House can therefore also be known as the Mother's House, the Parent or the Nurturer. Thinking about things from a more concrete point of view, we can see that the Fourth House also contains physical structures (houses) and real estate.

Family, history and traditions are reflected in the Fourth Chamber. All of these contribute to becoming a genuine, actualized, and individualized self. That's how we're coming home.

Fifth House

There are many ways to gain emotional satisfaction, and yet another way that this House is addressing is gambling. While this involves a financial risk, it can also be seen as the desire to take a risk— on love, money, or in life. How the Fifth House sees it is a gut risk in the hopes of a pleasurable outcome. This House is pretty rich in pleasures, because it also lord's fun, game.

The fifth house is the home of playfulness, joy, creativity, pleasure, and romance. This refers in all forms of play to your creative and spontaneous self-expression. As a child, what were you like? What makes you happy? With a love of gambling and speculation, inconstancy and exceptionally fickle affections are associated.

The interest in amusement and social activities may be rather exaggerated. Childhood is typically clearly defined, and marriage is highly likely to result in a large family. Children are also important in the Fifth House as a source of pleasure. This takes us back to creativity as we create an upgrade of ourselves through our children and then allow it to grow. It's certainly a pleasurable pursuit to give our kids all the good we had (and have), and some more. How is this going to emerge? What is the best form of fun and emotional release for our kids? Leo is the ruler of the fifth house, ruled by the ever-glowing sun, and his key phrase is "I will."

The Sixth House

The Sixth House is usually called the House of Health. The ability to cope with adversity is implicit in maintaining good health, and this theme is truer in the Sixth House. We naturally have deficiencies as human beings.

How are we going to react to a personal crisis? Crises, illnesses, and fate reversals are all part of our Earthly Journey. What we deal with these circumstances and the lessons they teach us inevitably helps to identify the person we become. Our doubts that hold us back, but if we can face them head-on and come out stronger on the other hand, we will learn the valuable service lesson or what the work of our life should be.

The Sixth House is centered on work and service. The attention here is on employment (employers and employees), training, serving us (along with those we serve) and relying on us. Here, too, it is essential to keep ourselves strong during these efforts, which is why this House continues to focus on health (good and bad), diet, exercise and hygiene. The work we do in life is essential to the work we do on our own.

Duty, obligation and personal development all contribute to the development of a fully realized being. We're working for others as well as ourselves; we're helping those who need us, including our own. There are times when health or faith crises are going to stand in the way of our best self.

At that time, we must strive to heal ourselves (again, this House's focus is on health) so that we can return to the work of acknowledging our potential for summing up, of serving our universe. The sixth house, governed by the resourceful Virgo, rules your daily life. It also dictates your awareness level and problem-solving skills. It covers your day-to-day duties, health habits and due care.

The sixth house also controls your domestic pets and their attitude towards habits, preparation, and organization. After all, the key phrase of Virgo is that of "I analyze." The Sixth House is also discussing the daily life: what am I going to wear today? Will I have a haircut? Did the dog get fed? These simple things keep our engines humming and allow us to do our choice's most important work. It's a quilt patchwork: the ability to serve others through health and work that is both useful and fulfilling.

The sixth house, run by resourceful Virgo, governs your daily life. It also determines the level of awareness and the ability to solve problems. It covers your day-to-day duties, health habits, and due care. The sixth house also controls your pets at home and your attitude towards habits, preparation, and organization.

After all, the key sentence of Virgo is "I'm analyzing." Service is likely to be the key to success, and the greatest benefits are produced by subordinate capability work. A possibility of some financial profit from inferiors, even though it is likely to be limited due to initiative and responsibility, and the best results will tend to come from under-directed work. The Sixth House is regulated by the Virgo Sign and the Planet Mercury.

The Seventh House

The Seventh House should be where we go beyond our particular concerns and take an interest in others, whether this is an interest in the general public or an interest in a particular person we are bonding with.

That's why this house has to do with relationships, obligations to someone besides ourselves. Popularity continues to bring popularity in all relations with the general public and leads to social success. Money or property can result from marriage, and partnerships are likely to be profitable. Probable public interest and the ability to deal with official positions. Any responsibility for damages in action.

The Seventh House is commonly called the Partnership House. We see from a different perspective away from the self to another— a partner with this House. We unite in order to achieve something by cooperating with and relating to another. The seventh house has to do with partnership: marriage, business partnerships, domestic partnerships, soulmates, and your disposition toward those unions. It also rules the enemy's freedom.

Under this house also come agreements, contracts and mediators like lawyers. This section of your chart is governed by Venus-ruled Libra, and its key sentence is "I Balance." The Seventh House's purpose is important— the act of having accomplished something big or small for the self, the relationship, and even the whole of society. We also become a more valued member of our community in uniting with another: we contribute, a tiny cog in the wheel of life.

We've got a purpose. Cooperation and partnership are helping to accelerate our life purpose. We fill our essential being through a partnership. Suddenly, in context, we see ourselves. We are fully established and completed through a partnership in which we work, play, love, and/or create. The other half is helping to make us whole.

The way we relate to others will undoubtedly help to define the success we have as a human being and as a member of humanity. The 7th House shows that many forms of partnerships, including marriages, business relations, contracts, laws, negotiations and contracts, are possible. We will cooperate more or fairly in these various partnerships. The quality of this cooperation is central to the Seventh House, and in essence how we deal with each other. Why are we doing this partnership? Is it because of love or money? Practical grounds? Socioeconomic considerations? There are plenty of reasons to unite with another. We can choose to fill in the voids that we see within ourselves.

We might just want another's company and companionship. The partnerships that we form say a lot about ourselves and also serve to teach us a lot. This House wants people to know that the standard of our partnerships is going to improve our lives, make them fuller, more special and better for all. Tensions also help to teach us lessons in a relationship. For this reason, the Seventh House concentrates on the darker side of our unions.

This House deals with divorce, legal proceedings and treaties. A partnership can create the worst of enemies, and these divisions can worsen into war on a more global scale. It is our response to this adversity that will shape the upcoming partnerships. The Sign Libra and the Planet Venus are in charge of the Seventh House.

The Eighth House

It has been said that the Eighth House is mainly concerned with sex, but this is too narrow a concept. This house has more to do with how we cut through the bureaucracy and get to the nitty-gritty right down to where things really are. This is where we strip the veneer away and get to the bare facts. It's more about business and essential exchanges than about sexuality. Possibility of inheritance money, or through mother, wife, or husband.

Many children are likely, but some of them could die. After marriage or litigation there may be some financial losses which greatly reduce the benefits derived from legacies. Significant respect that may be accorded after death. For example, an orgasm is a kind of miniature death; sexuality is regulated by this House.

It's also about rebirth, crisis and transition, addiction, redemption, recovery, and the attitudes towards those issues. It also governs your relationship with money from other people—the money you may be given after someone dies, the money from your partner and the money you owe to others (i.e. your debts and taxes). This portion of the map belongs to Scorpio dominated by Pluto, and its key phrase is "I wish."

The 8th House is commonly known as the House of Sex. This House dives deep into relationships— connections with another, and how some elements of those interactions can take on a more social character. This refers to what our relationships are going to bring us and how we should make the most of it.

Returning to the emphasis of this House on sex, it is important to remember that the French refer to an orgasm as' le petit mort' or' the little death.' When we get to that exalted state of communion, we leave behind a little bit of ourselves— die a minor death. One could also choose to interpret this as development, a new start, the soul's rebirth or a partnership benefit.

The Eighth House is a house of equal rights that puts race, death and rebirth on the same level playing field and acknowledges the potential and value of all three. As part of our lives we will all experience death and rebirth: failed relationships leading to new ones, career choices, a new haircut. With each new phase, we are transformed and reborn, and therefore should welcome them.

The Eighth House also has shared resources: property, alimony, income, insurance, assistance from another. The House addresses financial assistance, as well as social, emotional and physical support. While many of the aforementioned aspects are shared by our relationships, they will have their own dynamics and grow from within (we grow through our sexuality as well as other more measurable means).

That said, as broad as our relationships are, so do they even have other limitations, many that society places on them. Taxes, alimony and the common nature of assets once again come immediately to mind. Sure, we can face a restriction along with every opportunity that we have. Death and rebirth all over again. Rituals are illuminated in accordance with the changing essence of this Building.

That community has its own way to look deeply into the soul and the past, if only to get a sense of what we really are. What price do our rituals assume? High-ranking nations or metamorphoses? What secrets are we keeping, and why? It's critical for the Eighth House how we handle our interactions, relationships and routines— will we be truthful, successful and responsible? Will we be beneficial to the whole world (company, humanity) with our rich relationships? We have our story here: how we are doing now and how we are going to do it all the way. The Scorpio Sign and the Mars and Pluto Planets are ruling the Eighth Chamber.

The Ninth House

The House of Philosophy is commonly called the House of Ninth or The Ninth House According to this subject, our quest for meaning is an emphasis here.

Through discovering our universe, we begin to grasp what we have already at our fingertips. It all boils down to knowing: understanding what we see and hear in the hopes of discovering true meaning, and further searching. Whether it's theory or psychology, the Ninth House tells us we're on a discovery trip. We will be meeting our values along that path and defining the principles by which we live.

Another view to a clearer interpretation and understanding of what we see is through religion, and more importantly, that which we do not see. The Ninth House is key to understanding and acknowledging that which is greater than us and our universe. Sadly, in the face of what we have, we may not always be modest.

A realistic perception of life's possibilities may well contribute to selfish greed and covetousness, and self-expansion. They enact laws to tackle those forces most efficiently in society. These laws provide for that society to grow orderly and positively. Philosophy and faith relate in much the same way to putting attention and purpose into a productive society. The core tenets of the Ninth House are how members of a society relate, and knowledge and respect of the laws by which they live.

The Ninth House also addresses the way we extend our inner and outer lives. A way to this end is travel and contact with other peoples and cultures. It's possible that there's a great deal of interest in religious and philosophical topics, with mysticism learning. In general, creativity is good, and tends to promote mental change. The individual often experiences rare vivid dreams.

Much travel, especially by sea, is likely and will likely be gain-productive. Publicity can be person-centered, likely in connection with a religious opinion shift that causes extreme censorship. Impulse and overhasty assumptions can create travel difficulties. Our visions, those that reflect our history and those that refer to future events, are also helping to shape our being and our relationships. Taking this one step further, psychics too come into play as the bearers of relevant information.

In addition, the Ninth House deals with publishing and international businesses such as import / export firms. The House also has a multigenerational view, taking into consideration all grandchildren and the in-laws. The Ninth Room, though, is most philosophically inclined to look for meaning and reality at the end of the day. The Ninth Chamber is governed by the Sign of Sagittarius and Planet Jupiter.

Tenth House

Popularity and prosperity in public ventures are likely to result from success. Feminine curiosity is likely to be stimulated, and success usually comes from the public-related professions at large. Thrift helps greatly in property development although there may be some benefits from outside sources. Reversals of wealth, scandal and public censorship may result from conditions that are unfavorable. It is possible that there will be a strong interest in religious and philosophical topics, with a learning of mysticism. In general, imagination is strong, and tends to enable mental change. The individual sometimes experiences extremely vivid dreams. Much travel is likely, particularly by sea, and is likely to be gain-productive. Publicity can be person-centred, likely in connection with a religious opinion shift that causes extreme censorship. Impulse and overhasty conclusions can create travel difficulties.

The Tenth House is usually called the House of Social Status. It's about the point we've reached in our social (or work / career) class, and in the whole of society. Think status, the power it conveys and hence the role we play in our society. It also refers to any endorsements that we earn, any recognition that we may or may have, and the types of business and social events that we engage in.

The House is reflecting on how we see ourselves and how the world as a whole views us (and our efforts) in terms of achievement. We're working on manifesting ourselves through this Building. Vocation at Tenth House is important Which position are we going to choose and how are we going to best fill that? How much to accomplish? Here is where career, professional goals, ambition and motivation come into play.

Employers and their rules are covered here in a more practical context, as are any other organizations (specifically the government) that are able to rule over us. The burden of ruling over others comes along with the work of our life, though there will usually be someone lording over us. The prestige and social status we are gaining by virtue of our careers and professions can be seen in the form of ego gratification, intangibly.

The tenth house deals with how we manage this. In our consumerist society, it can be most difficult to tire of financial rewards; shockingly, ego massage may grow older faster. The topic of how we treat these gifts, and the prestige that comes with them, is important to this Chamber.

Are we going to use our influence to really help society or are we going to be dishonest and reckless? Not all of us are cut out for social success on a grand scale or ready to dramatically help society. It's also important to take note that with the help of the society, many of our successes are achieved, not in a vacuum. The individual's relationship to a group and with society is also highlighted in the Tenth House. We must feel a real kinship to the cause to better things and make an impact; a fervent determination to change things is important. We will gain the social status that really is worthwhile in this way. Eventually, the Tenth House addresses the father, who is usually the more authoritarian parent, in keeping with his emphasis on rulers. The Sign Capricorn and Planet Saturn reign over the Tenth Chamber.

The Eleventh House

In conjunction with communities, associations and clubs, a wide range of friends brings recognition and success. Women tend to play a considerable part in life. However, there is a probability of danger from self-seeking friends who presume to pursue their own ambitions with friendship.

The Eleventh Building is commonly known as Friends ' Hall. We find strength in numbers of our mates— we see the power of collective, community. The House's target groups include parties, unions, social groups, networking and professional associations. The emphasis here is on the tasks within these communities that we pursue, how we make a difference, and as a result, how we develop and actualize our true self.

Therefore, it is the community that helps to determine what we as individuals are going to do by virtue of its collective power. Our conversations and endeavors are in line with our life priorities; these interactions have the ability to make our lives better. A Love Work? Yes, in a whole lot of ways. By our experiences with friends and communities we add substance and meaning to our lives and to society.

The Eleventh House often refers to life— in simpler terms, our hopes and dreams, what we have to do and what we want to accomplish. It highlights our creative vision, the simple act of working towards our maximum selves. The power of collective production is also essential to this House as are the innovative sparks created by the community. We can create so much more, by banding together.

We not only achieve a great deal in meeting our mates, but we can also reap the benefits of our labor. The Eleventh House is also discussing the kind of friend that we are: what are we doing for others? Why do we see our friends that way? We also work towards a greater good through our families, and in the hope of improving society. This is our charitable side which comes to the fore, the ability to help others with eagerness and selflessness. It is also manifesting itself most effectively in our humanity. At times we that disrupt the proverbial apple cart, and it should be the sum total of our efforts to look at the end result. If that's successful then the cost of getting there is worthwhile, for better or for worse.

Last but not least, the Eleventh House also rules stepchildren, fosters children and adopts children. The Sign Aquarius, and the Planets Saturn and Uranus rule the Eleventh Chamber.

The Twelfth House

The Twelfth House is usually called the Unconscious House. The unconscious mind will help to bring about our achievements, as well as help us deal with our defeats. Progress vs. failure: do we face our lives knowingly, or subconsciously sweep stuff under the proverbial rug? This House could be called the House of Reckoning more accurately, as it is in the Twelfth where we examine what we have done (and are doing) and decide where we are going from there. They also ponder along with these unconscious musings on the strengths and weaknesses that are hidden from public view. The subconscious is working hard for us, trying to make sense of the lives.

This shadow play is long and slow, and frequently full of fear and pain. It is in this sense that we face our sorrows, pain and the lies that we hold from ourselves and others. In the end, we're all faced with our fate: destiny. Today, we follow the outcomes of all we have achieved. This also concentrates on the repressed interests and limits them. What have we done in our lives with?

This is the Twelfth House's key issue and we will be grappling with it both consciously and unconsciously. Will the answers force us to turn ourselves or reborn again? This is another pillar of the Twelfth House— the way we grow. We will learn a great deal from the subconscious. We will be inspired to be generous at its noblest manifestation.

Unless we learn our lessons, past as well as present, then we are also better equipped to progress. The Twelfth House is pushing us to pursue spiritual closure as an aid to solid growth. The zodiac's last House also acknowledges that we can feel bound in life— stuck and confined. This House therefore governs prisons, hospitals, schools, asylums and any room inhibiting expression. Further darkness in the Twelfth comes in the form of risk, covert activities and hidden enemies. Watch out! While some might describe the Twelfth House as the zodiac's garbage bin, it is truly an unfair term. This House, in the end, is the champion of positive transformations. It is here that we are standing on the precipice and deciding how we are going to proceed.

We begin to pick up what the future will bring by visiting the unconscious and interacting with the past. Home life, such as nursing, jail service, or charitable work, appears to be preferred or an occupation requiring seclusion. There is a duty to engage in secret love affairs though they do not always need to be catastrophic. It would seem that the major danger is deception, deep enmity and treachery. The Twelfth House is governed by the Planets and the Sign Pisces.

CHAPTER SIX:
All Of The Planets As A Whole

The universe is so big, but most times, people do not realize because humans only know the world they are born into. There exist nine planets in the world; Mercury, Venus, Earth, Mars, Jupiter, Saturn, Uranus, Neptune and Pluto. As an astrologer, it is important to know some things about other planets.

You must be curious, one of the characteristics of being an astrologer that you must have is being inquisitive. Now, these nine planets are going to be discussed extensively which will give you insight on some things you've never heard about before. Sit back and enjoy the ride into an entirely different part of the universe. The original art goes beyond your own horoscopes.

They exist other part of the universe that are sometimes also referred to planets and they are two and are called 'the moon' and 'the sun'; other times, they are classified as celestial bodies and these asteroids have different roles they play on our plane; Earth. It just really provides you with very useful information when you know the dynamics of the universe. Astrology majorly uses the actions and associations of the planets to determine what will have impact in our lives.

I earlier mentioned that there were nine planets but in recent times, Astrologers have done research and classified both the sun and the moon as a planet. In the study of Astrology, we look at ten planets, starting with the Sun and the Moon, also referred to as 'the lights or luminaries'. Furthermore, there are others; Mercury, Venus, Mars, Jupiter, Saturn, Uranus, Neptune and Pluto as earlier mentioned. Mercury, Venus, Earth, and Mars are often classified as terrestrial planets, Jupiter and Saturn are called the 'gas giants', Uranus and Neptune are the ice giants, while Pluto is a dwarf planet. In order to identify whether a celestial object can be listed as a planet, three rules are applied.

The IAU; International Astronomical Union which was founded in 1919 have stated this three rules: The planet must be an orbit that revolves round the Sun Has enough mass to withstand rigid body forces in order to take on a hydrostatic equilibrium (practically round) form and The area around its orbit is cleared. It is believed that there are signs that these Planets operate on; Sign of dignity, Sign of exaltation, sign of detriment, Sign of fall.

The Sign of dignity talks about the way each planets place force and go to extreme to govern with strong force involving the Sign it is attached to. The Sign of detriment which is the opposite of the Sign of dignity helps us understand that whatever Planet that falls under this is usually unfavourable. The Sign of exaltation talks on how Planets relate with each other.

Finally, the opposite of Sign of exaltation which is the Sign of fall have the planets operate on energy so weak. Planetary movement is defined as fixed, forward or backward. There will be highly focused and substantial energy in a stationary world; which will eventually be either backwards or forward and there is also significant influence on neighbouring planets. The Planets that tend to cause mix up are the ones moving backwards, they most times produce diffused and confused energy just by being Retrograde Planets. As a result, the retrograde planets ' communication will be confused and less successful. Elements signify either simple or complicated possibilities and circumstances that occur in life. Good aspects deliver good possibilities or conditions; whereas terrible / tough aspects generate challenging situations.

But in life, they don't hold us back or hinder success. It is called aspects of structural connection between planets. Such partnerships influence and alter the planet's resources in question. Several aspects are said to create troublesome events in our lives, while others tend to simplify the direction with respect to the places controlled by the planets, signs and properties in question.

If a planet has challenging parts or is restless in the zodiac, it is said to be corrupted. The harmful features can be expressed in times by undesirable characteristics, or by tough situations in your life. Nevertheless, if it has beneficial aspects, the results will be more favourable. Hard aspects are often very troublesome and can even be disastrous in their consequences, in particular for the ' malignant ' (hazardous) Planets.

Obviously, they are more beneficial to self-improvement as they generally produce abstract findings requiring extensive comprehension and analysis on individuals, whereas beneficial aspects frequently produce straightforward effects that are understandable. In any event, the chart must be seen in its entirety so that, depending on the situation, both positive and negative characteristics can either be altered or in alleviated forms. The charts pattern will be fully explained in the next chapter but let us not drift away from the topic here, we are quickly going to dive into the main course.

SUN (Helios/Sol)

Sun also known Helios (Greek) or Sol (Italian) has the greatest mass in our solar system and is the full system's weight and principal source of heat and illumination which takes 99.86 percent out of 100% total mass.

It is mainly made of hydrogen and helium but also consists of oxygen, carbon, neon and iron. The process 'Thermonuclear fusion' which produces electromagnetic radiation which helps in the heating up of Earth that makes it possible for humans to live in, was caused during the formation of Sun when it became increasingly hot and dense thereby causing ignition and thus, conception of the Sun. Our planet was only a thick molecular cluster in our cosmos at the beginning of the solar system. But then an occurrence broke out, which isn't really explainable, and that occurrence led to the cloud to breaking down on its own.

Immediately the cloud exploded, the matter inside this cloud began to merge into one large mass and as this mass started growing, it spun at an increasing rate, creating a gravitational field around itself, pulling in more matter. A phenomenon called thermonuclear fusion took place in the middle of the solar system once it reached its maximum mass, rendering it a blazing object. The thermonuclear fusion method that sustains our sun is quite straightforward.

Two or more atomic nuclei make contact at extremely high speeds to produce a single nucleus at close proximity. This effectively allows hydrogen to transform to helium 4, which provides the solar system with extreme heat and electricity. To order to implement a secure energy source, scientists have attempted to replicate this cycle, which is why the hydrogen bombs were used, but they couldn't find a way to regulate it.

Therefore, for a while, only the stars have this sort of technology licensed. To our understanding, the sun has four essential layers but no solid mass. The heart of the process is that of thermonuclear fusion and it takes place in 'Core'. The core's density is 150 times that of water and exceeds 15 000 000 ° C in temperatures. The rotation of the core is quicker than the surface of the sun, which gives the sun its gravitational force.

The Radiative Zone is the region around the core which, as opposed to convective means, is the key means of transferring the energy created in the core. At this stage, the temperature drops mildly to around 5 000 000 ° C. Molecules in the radiative zone transfer energy to each other as they are triggered by heat and "bumping". Tachocline or Interface Layer is a tiny layer or transition region separating the radiative zone from the convective zone.

In this layer, the magnetic field of the sun is created by the process of magnetic dynamo. Research has shown that while the convective zone is accelerating its rotation, the radiative zone is decelerating and the tachocline tends to be the "void" between them. This rotational disparity between the two zones produces a Tachocline magnetic field and is likely the source of the frequency of 11-year sunspot cycles and cosmic rays. There is little clear with this section of the sun at this time, but studies are still gaining a better knowledge of all its function. The Convective Zone is the sun's outermost region where energy moves through convection.

The convection process is relatively easy to explain. As the molecules heat up, they lose mass, moving farther from each other and rising to the cooler regions, whereas, the fewer hot molecules are moving in their position and heating up, too. Immediately these molecules grow to cooler regions, they tend to cool down and compact again to sink deeper to the heat source.

This method creates a cycle of growing heated molecules and dropping cooled molecules. A good example of this is boiling water and ocean currents. Each year the Sun passes through each sign of the zodiac for about one month. It shows out what we want out of life. The Sun is the life-giver, radiating vitality, strength, self-awareness, curiosity and intelligence. The Sun's warm rays may, however, be used for both good and ill. This produces ego, resentment, conceit and selfishness when adversely affected.

The Sun is in relation to the conscious mind. Sun's atmosphere is also made up of three layers; The Photosphere, the Chromosphere, and the Corona.

Photosphere

Photosphere penetrates deep into the sun's atmosphere and the only part we can see is around 100-400 km thick (62.1 mi-248.5 mi). This is the sun's "solid" limit that we cannot see past and is less dense than the Earth's atmosphere, around 0.01 percent. This portion of the sun hits temperatures from 5000 to 8000° C, which is cooler than the other atmospheric layers of the Sun.

Chromosphere

It is much hotter than the extension of the photosphere from the mass of the sun. It is roughly 1500 km (932 mi) thick and crosses 4000° C temperatures as high when 25000° C as it passes into the Corona. The chromosphere is 0.01percent even less dense than the photosphere and can only be seen in total solar eclipses. It is also the red ring in the eclipse around the moon.

Corona

Corona; which extends several million kilometres around the sun and is also noticeable throughout solar eclipses, is the hottest (between 1 and 2 million° C) and the furthest point of the earth. It is the white light circling the moon during most of the eclipse and is 0.01 percent even less dense than the chromosphere. The Sun is generally believed to be about 4.6 billion years old and what is known as a yellow dwarf.

We have billions of years to go until the end of the life of the sun but scientists have speculated on what will happen when this process takes place in three phases; phase one- As the sun go running out of fuel, it will grow in size and transform from a yellow dwarf to a red giant. As it increases in size, all planets; Mercury, Venus, and Earth are consumed in close orbit.

Phase two- Once the sun approaches its peak size and transforms into a red giant, it then begins to emit bursting particles throughout the solar system that might force other particles and planets out of their orbit to cause mayhem throughout the system. And these particles will turn into what is called a nebula; which is the interstellar cloud of dust, hydrogen, helium and other ionized gasses.

Phase Three- This is when our sun is going to turn into a white dwarf. It's essentially a cold star that can't fuse within its core. It will effectively stop creating heat or light, so any remaining bodies or planets in its orbit will not be able to exist. There are many lingering questions, for example why Corona is the most heated point when it's so far away, but we can't get close enough to analyse and learn the answers to these questions due to the extreme heat.

For now, to tell us the mysteries of the sun, we rely on spectroscopes and infrared images. Maybe later on, we may find the ability to travel as near as possible to the sun to get a better view of the life blood of the solar system. Sun reflects the self, personality, ego, spirit and what makes a person special. It is our voice and the world's image.

The Sun often talks about the individual's creative ability and strength to deal with the issues of daily life. The energy of the Sun is a strong one, and leadership, the ability to lead and the essence of a person, their core being, falls into its wake. We aspire to develop ourselves in the universe through this planet's power. Sun is glorious, and it controls royalty and higher office in accordance with its royal air. This orb rules our health and well-being as well.

The golden glow of the Sun is a valuable life force that impregnates us with power, energy, and determination to succeed. It is the Sun that gives support to the other planets, which is why in Astrology this planet plays an important role. The Sun follows each Sign for about a month and involves a year to pass through the Zodiac's twelve Signs. It's male power, and Leo and the Fifth House rule.

MOON (Luna)

The satellite of Earth which is called the Moon (Luna), is a vital portion of our Planets oceanic systems which determines the tides and currents. Various theories exist on how the moon was created but astrologists accept the theory that concludes that Earth collides with 'Theia'; another planetary body thereby causing a wide piece of rock to be raised to the orbit by the force of Earth's gravity.

The rotational speed has given it its present "spherical" shape over time, which classifies it as a planet, not just a moon. The moon, when it's there, is the simplest celestial object to find in the night sky. The only natural satellite on Earth orbits brilliantly and round up in the sky until it seems to have vanished for a few hours.

For years, the cycle of the phases of the moon has driven humanity— for example, lunar months are about the same as the time required to go from one full moon to the other. For many, the moon phases and the orbit of the moon are philosophical questions. The moon always shows everyone the same face, for instance. That's because spinning on its axis and orbiting Earth takes 27.3 days. We really see the full moon, half-moon or no moon; new moon, because sunlight is reflected by the moon.

How much we see depends on the situation of the moon with respect to Earth and the sun. While Earth's shadow, the moon is larger than Pluto, with a diameter of approximately 2,159 miles (3,475 kilometres). (Four other planets are already larger in our solar system.) The moon is a quarter of the Earth, a much smaller percentage (1:4) than any other planet and its planets. This means that now the moon has a tremendous impact on the planet and that's what makes the whole thing possible on Earth. The primary theory for how the moon was created was that a massive explosion kicked off the fragile molten Earth and into space for the moon's fresh ingredients.

Scientists proposed that the asteroid was about 10% of the Earth's mass, almost the size of Mars. Since Earth and the moon are so similar in nature, scholars have estimated that after the evolution of the universe, the collision must have happened around 95 million years, giving or taking 32 million years. New studies in 2015 gave more strength to this theory, centred on simulations of planetary orbits in the early universe, and also recently discovered differences. In 2015, new research brought more weight to this hypothesis, based on models of planetary orbits in the early solar system, along with recently discovered variations in the concentration of the tungsten-182 element observed in Earth and the moon.

So, while the theory of great impact controls the conversation of the scientific community, there are many other ideas for the formation of the moon. These include that, according to a current concept, the Earth captured the moon, that the moon fission from the Earth, or that Earth just might have stolen the moon from Venus. The moon will probably have a very small core, just 1 to 2 percent of the mass of the moon and about 680 km (420 miles) long. It is typically mainly made of iron, but it could also contain large quantities of sulphur and other elements. The volcanic mantle is about 825 miles (1,330 km) dense and consists of solid iron and magnesium-rich minerals.

In the past, magmas in the mantle came to light and erupted volcanically for over a billion years— from at least four billion years ago to less than three billion years ago. On top, the layer measures around 70 km (42 miles) thick. Because of all the huge effects it has provided, the outermost portion of the crust is fractured and cluttered, a fragmented region that gives way to solid material under a depth of about 6 miles (9.6 km). The moon is rugged, like the four inner planets. It's littered millions of years ago with craters created by asteroid impacts. The craters have not fractured because there is no climate. The lunar surface's total composition by weight is about 43% oxygen, 20% carbon, 19% magnesium, 10% iron, 3% calcium, 3% aluminium, 0.42% chromium, 0.18% titanium and 0.12% manganese. Orbiters also found signs of deep underground water on the lunar surface.

We have found hundreds of boxes that could accommodate long-term explorers on the moon. Continuing measurements from the Lunar Reconnaissance Orbiter (LRO) have shown that water is more plentiful on slopes facing the southern lunar pole, while scientists note that it is similar to an extremely dry desert. In the meantime, a report in 2017 indicated that the interior of the moon might also be rich in salt. The moon has a really dense atmosphere, so for millennia a coating of soil, or a footprint, will remain undisturbed. Yet, heat is not kept close to the surface without even an atmosphere, so temperatures vary enormously.

On the sunny side of the moon, daytime temperatures reach 273 degrees F (134 C); on the dark side it becomes as chilly as less than 243 F (minus 153 C). The moon's average distance from Earth: 225,700 miles (363,300 km), Apogee (farthest distance from Earth): 252,000 miles (405,500 km), Orbit circumference: 1,499,618.58 miles (2,413,402 km), Mean orbit speed: 2,287 mph (3,680.5 km / h).

MERCURY

Is the nearest to the sun, and it is the second smallest planet in our solar system, with only 88 days of rotation around the sun. The planet's surface approaches temperatures as high as 840 ° F in the day and hundreds of degrees just under the freezing point at night due to its close contact to the celestial giant.

Because of the high conditions, there is no atmosphere, so the floor of the earth is riddled with pock marks and asteroid impact craters. Mercury comes in on feather-light wings, much like the winged messenger of the gods, and instructs us to speak. Interaction, intellect and awareness are all inside the domain of Mercury, including logic and reasoning and how we build and express our thinking processes. A mercurial arrangement brings restlessness and motion to mind. Mercury is about a quick wit, fast thinking, possibilities, ideas, reasoning, and the ability to streamline things. Mercurial energy can be positive or negative, but it promises to be amazing. This planet also pushes us to move from place to place and it responds to all our inquisitiveness; Physically as well as psychologically. In addition, the energy of Mercury is both dexterous and perceptive.

Mercury is all about short rides; a city-wide tour to a neighbour or a friend, a weekend getaway. Siblings, as well as travel in general, are also in the realm of Mercury. This planet urges us to express ourselves frequently — and well. However, when Mercury goes backwards, our communications will be threatened. Mercury never comes from the Sun more than 28 degrees; it requires about 88 days to complete the Sun's orbit. It is neither male nor female and it also refers to the identity of the Symbol it is in. It governs the Third and Sixth Houses as well as the Virgo and Gemini.

VENUS

Venus; this poisonous earth, consisting mainly of carbon dioxide, will be first in line with the sun and holds an index of gravity which could kill anyone walking on its surface.

Although it is far away from the sun than Mercury, Venus is the solar system's hottest planet and can be seen from the Earth's human eye. The world is enveloped by a thick cloud, making it tough to see its atmosphere equating its brightness. Venus has been discovered since the dawn of time in the skies of Earth.

Because of its reflective nature and closeness to Earth, it was named after the goddess of love and beauty by the Romans as the sharpest and brightest planet in our solar system. It is our solar system's sixth largest planet and is situated just 25 million miles (40 million km) from Earth. Closely related in size, density, composition, and volume as Earth, in geology and environment it is often referred to as the twin sister of Earth and thought to be suitable for life.

The Mariner 2 probe did show us in 1962 that Venus was in fact the evil twin of Earth with an unfitting harsh environment to sustain life. Where Earth is Eden's Garden, Venus is Hell's Bowels. Venus is 41.84 million kilometres from the sun (67.24 million miles). This revolves around the sun after 225 Earth Days, but what is fascinating is that its pole rotation is faster than its 243 Earth Times rotation around the sun. So, it basically takes 8 months for the sun to rise and fall on Venus every day, which makes it very sluggish opposed to Earth, but only takes 7 months to spin around the sun. The major reason for Venus' slow rotation on its axis is that it cannot keep a magnetic field to shield it from the sun's solar winds.

Venus does have a reverse rotation on its axis opposed to Earth's, allowing the sun to rise in the west and set in the east, while Earth rises and sets in the east and West respectively. Scientists suggest that this abnormality might have been caused by the effect of a planet-sized object in its ancient history with Venus reversing its rotation and pulling it down.

Its orbit remains quite constant as it rotates, keeping it close to the heat and light of the sun. However, weather patterns and such remain fairly constant on a daily basis and for certain parts of the planet there really is no "relief" during the course of the year. Almost nothing is known about the inner structure of Venus.

It is assumed that it may have a partly molten core, a rocky mantle, and a crust owing to its many ties to Earth. At this time, however, this is all hearsay because pressure on Venus has decelerated the research of its surface as well as internal structure. If you stood on the surface, you would experience a big difference in the planet's gravitational pull and friction if you could live long enough.

A person on Earth weighing 68 kg (150 lbs) will reduce the weight of Venus to just 26 kg (57 lbs). The tension on the planet is similar to diving 1000 meters straight into the ocean of the Earth, the human body can only handle the pressures at about 500 meters. It is concluded that it may have been on a similar route in the development of Earth at some period in the initial beginnings of Venus. Granite was found on the surface of the planet suggesting that water could have been on the soil at one point.

Yet, that water there had evaporated ages ago due to the extreme heat. Thereby, leaving this planet bereft of moisture to cool the magma that is spewing on the surface or offset the CO2 that is constantly gathering within its atmosphere. Even though in many ways, Venus is similar to Earth, its geology is quite distinct. Riddled with incredibly active volcanoes, alone, 167 are more than 100 km (62 miles) across, covering the surface with lava fields, hard jagged rocks, and practically no water. There is another danger in this severe terrain that is also deadly for any living organisms. As bad as Venus might look, in the confusion of our sister planet, there is grace and hope.

For many reasons, scientists today are researching Venus thoroughly, but mostly to develop an understanding of what the future of Earth could mean if greenhouse gasses are not regulated. Some scientists have already suggested that due to its close proximity to Earth, the colonization of Venus might be more possible than Mars, making travel far simpler and less time wasting. All propositions have been rejected so far, though. Then again, no one wants to move to hell.

EARTH

Earth is the Sun's third planet and the only astronomical element that embraces life. Earth formed more than 4.5 billion years ago, as per radiometric dating and other outlets of evidence. The Planet we live on; Earth, is the only identified planet to share the atmosphere with primitive organisms. Our small little world, rich in rivers and lakes, mountains and valleys, teams of life and diverse ecosystems.

Simply known as Earth, Gaia in Greek, and Terra in Latin, there are several factors that make life possible. With the farthest distance of 152 million km (94.5 million miles) and the nearest distance of 147 million km (91.4 million miles) from the sun, the elliptical orbit of Earth causes heating up and cooling down; seasons, to take place. This, along with a few other factors, is essential for life to happen.

The complete rotation of Earth around the sun takes about 365 days and the Earth's axial tilt of 23.5 allows each of the poles to spend some time in the sun as it revolves on its axis for the full spin at about 24 hours. The thing we about our planet's internal structure is centred on theories extracted from the unintended study of geological characteristics such as lava fields and sediment layers. The farthest we've reached into the centre of our Planet is about 12.3

km (7.6 miles), Kola Superdeep Borehole, and Earth's heart is around 6,371 km (3,958 miles). So really, we still have to grasp the basics of what lies over and above our planet's crust let alone the various layers below.

The geography of Earth is as varied as its substance. It's made of hills, rivers, lakes, fields, valleys and more. The main geography of Earth is water about 71%. 96.5% of the Earth's water is stored in its vast oceans which lets the atmosphere sustain normal Earth temperatures. When the water gets hot, the atmosphere evaporates and gets trapped. It cools down in the atmosphere and comes back to the surface to refill the supply of water which helps to cool the surface temperature. Since the Earth's tectonic plates are dynamic, as they are constantly moving, there are regular seismic changes.

They are seeing this in worldwide volcanic eruptions, floods, tsunamis as well as other natural disasters. Such events cause minute changes over thousands of years in our surface structure, but they are constant and make the planet's geology constantly alter. So, what can be true today, 1000 years from now, it may not occur.

The atmosphere on Earth consists of 78% nitrogen, 21% oxygen, traces of water vapour, carbon dioxide, and several other gasses. The approach helps us to have clean air while removing the greater portion of the solar radiation that might harm the earth and its inhabitants. This is also a secondary "shield" that protects the Earth from space debris.

The magnetic field primarily deflects solar radiation that can "fry" our earth literally, but our atmosphere shields us from threats like asteroids and meteors. Alone, the shock waves, as a result of the effect of such objects may cause major occurrences such as destroying all life within or globally in a general area.

However, as it goes through our atmosphere, most of these objects are shattered and disintegrated before landfall occurs. The Earth has just one satellite called the Moon (Lunar). It has not many geological features and has no surface activity. Our own planet's discovery is non-stop. In all fields, Scientists are constantly on guard in studying our planet's various aspects. Thorough research on the interior of the Earth has been there since the late 1900's.

In order to learn the system of geological alterations that mold our planet, natural occurrence like volcanic eruptions are constantly noted. Even astronomical research is carried out on other planetary objects to fully understand our world and how unique it really is. The thinnest layer, the crust, is the layer on which we live, and is about 40 km (25 miles) thick. It is the planet's hard rocky area that allows us to grow crops, hold the surface water, and basically walk around on. It consists of a rock mostly hardened with silicate.

- The next layer is about 2.900 km broad and is called the mantle. The mantle consists of two separate layers of hardened silicate rock predominantly within itself. There is the inner cloak and the outer cloak.
- The outer shell is much heavier than the main mantle, rendering it much solider. It is the layer between the inner mantle more viscous and thinner, and the crust.

- The inner mantle, like gravel on a humid day, is much less firm. It moves extremely slowly, even more slowly and thickly than lava or a bowl of hot oatmeal.
- Then finally there's the core. Like the mantle, this section of the planet also has two layers.
- The outer core is shaped to the liquid point. It is where the cooler iron and nickel elements rotate at a slower rate than the inner core in a western direction.
- The inner core comprises of strong iron and nickel. This section of the centre shifts in an easterly direction at a super-fast rotation. The opposing movement at different speeds is what produces both our gravitational and magnetic fields in the centre of the Earth, creating a positive and negative effect. This process is referred to as the geomagnetic dynamo.

Which creates our magnetic field, atmosphere, and winds on the surface of the planet, helping to keep the surface temperature of the Earth and keeping everything on the ground. If that procedure were to take place. The atmosphere of Earth retains its heat, making surface temperatures warmer for plants to grow while allowing sufficient heat to escape to keep things from getting too hot. The combination of nitrogen and oxygen helps to keep the carbon dioxide levels down and, if not kept in check, will cause a heating effect. That's what they call the greenhouse effect and it's what killed off any life chances on Venus.

Earth's temperatures differ according to location as well as season. In Antarctica the coldest temperatures ever recorded on the planet were-89.2° C (-128.56 ° F). The hottest temperatures ever recorded in Iran's Lut Desert in 2005 were 70.7° C (159.26° F). Greenhouse gasses in the atmosphere such as CO_2 tend to regulate the temperature on the surface of the planet by "holding" the heat and not enabling it to disperse into space. Without them, Earth would not be able to keep the heat that is needed to sustain life.

MARS

This is the Sun's fourth planet and the second smallest planet following Mercury in the Solar System. Mars bears the name of the Roman god of war in English and is sometimes called the ' Red Planet '. It has a perihelion at 206 million km (128 million miles) and an aphelion at 248 million km (154 million miles), but significantly more than Earth from the sun at a distance of 228.5 million km (142 million miles).

The elliptical orbit causes it to get the same seasons as Earth does, which gives it the exact surface heating and cooling effect. At the perihelion, its southern polar region faces the sun, while its northern polar region faces the aphelion. This is because Mars is revolving on an axis (at an angle of 25 °) like Earth. This gives Mars optimal conditions for the hope of future colonization, although not flawless.

The rotation of Mars around the sun takes 687 days compared to Earth's 365 days. It results in higher temperatures in the summer and colder temperatures in the winters on the surface of Mars than on Earth. However, its seasonal correlation to Earth is one of the main reasons why Mars was properly considered capable of managing a colony on its surface. The outer crust of Mars is created out of a basaltic rock similar to that of Earth.

A fine surface of iron-high dust encompasses the crust, which gives the planet an infamous red colour, but below it is a greyish-blue rock. It is suspected that Mars, very much like Earth's, may also have a silicate rock mantle, but it is not yet fully understood. Scientists are trying to ascertain whether their core consists of a compound of iron and nickel just like the core of Earth, or whether or not the core of Mars has the same liquid and solid state. Without any magnetic field covering the earth, there is a strong view that this is most certainly not due to the need for the planet to establish a magnetic field.

The geography of Mars is very identical to that of Earth and may have once found to contain flowing water on the surface, but this water would've been evaporated by billions of years of disclosure to solar winds without a magnetic field long time ago. Water, however, remains in frozen state within its polar regions and periodically melts to flow throughout the layer. In the run-off lines that extend across the earth, the signs of this, and typographic images show various particles littering some regions that can only be seen with the presence of water. All of that, apart from plant and animal life, is not part of its geography is it doesn't include oceans.

Although latest research has shown that underneath the surface, water can flow, which could only have prevented solidification if it contained salt, a component usually found in oceans. Since Mars has no magnetic field to save humanity from the radiation of suns, billions of years of attack from toxic "solar winds" have destroyed almost all of the protective layers of the planet. Everything that exists is a toxic, polluted atmosphere comprising 96% carbon dioxide and just 0.2% oxygen. The atmosphere, however, which is 100 times less dense than that of the Earth's, maintains the surface wind ability and its 25° axial rotation giving the planet seasons. Unlike any planet in our solar system, Mars has phases of great storms of dust.

Such large storms may last weeks and cover areas of continent scale. These storms are so severe that they could be seen from Earth through the use of telescopes and are known to cover the whole planet at times (about every three years). They are often not, however, as fatal as people can think of their size. Due to the dense atmosphere on Mars, the largest wind force that would occur is about 97 km (60 miles) per hour, which is hardly half the wind force an Earth's hurricane. The pollution coating the earth is very small, clinging to it all. An article on NASA's website Trip to Mars states that "Mars dust particles are very small and slightly electrostatic, so they stick to the surfaces they contact like peanuts packed with Styrofoam."

It could cause a major problem since solar power could be the major source of power on the planet if inhabited as well as the solar panels required constant cleaning to keep the solar rays obtained. Like Earth, temperatures on the surface of Mars differ significantly according to the location and season on the surface of the planets. During the summer days, temperatures vary from -133 ° C (-207 ° F) to 27 ° C (80 ° F).

The distance between Mars and the sun doesn't really permit it to reach higher temperatures and also, there is zero greenhouse effect to keep the heat on the layer, so the extreme temperatures of Mars are relatively moderate. Mars contains two asteroids that are thought to have been seized. Several unmanned missions to Mars have been going on since the 1960s. Their initial goal was to prove that life exists on the surface of the planet.

Nevertheless, after it was established that there was no life on the layer; which could be easily determined, missions slowed down quite a bit because financing decreased as a result of the frustration of finding no life. Currently, a variety of agencies and governmental organizations are pushing for Mars' colonization by 2020 at the latest.

Theories have been initiated for how we can make Mars more habitable, like, for example, stuffing the planet with oxygen-producing microbes, but definitive plans haven't been made yet. Over the past 50 years, several schemes have emerged to send a colony to Mars, some of which are operated secretly, like the

Mars One Project. Mars, the God of War, symbolizes confidence, power, endurance, perseverance and physical energy.

This offers the virtues of bravery, frankness, strength and ambition. Mars is a reflection of your strength and attractiveness. It's better for people inspired by Mars to do something than to schedule them.

JUPITER

Is the Sun's fifth planet and the Solar System's biggest. It is a gas giant one and a half times that of all the other planets in the solar system with one and one-thousandth of Sun mass. Jupiter has an enormous diameter of 133,708 km, which implies you might bring the Earth into Jupiter and still have enough room for other things. Because of the extraordinary magnetic field of Jupiter, it is technically impossible for any living person to get close enough to examine the planet's titan. So much we learn, instead of empirical facts, is based on assumption and intuition. Jupiter is the planet of the thinking person.

As the keeper of the creative mind, this world governs higher learning and offers us a passion for the intellectual and spiritual pursuit of concepts. Jupiter allows us to shape our philosophy scientifically. In the most sacred world Jupiter's rulers' beliefs and ideology. Jupiter suggests that you search for responses and that is probably why Jupiter regulates long distance travel when it means spanning the globe to find them.

Jupiter compels us to evaluate our ethical and moral values in accordance with this theme; it also addresses our sense of optimism. The gravity of Jupiter alone, a whopping 24.79 compared to Earth's 9.8, together with its immense magnetosphere, is one of the most impressive aspects of this giant planet. Every entity that enters the Earth is torn apart by the magnetosphere of the world, and it inevitably crushes anything that tries to enter its clouds.

Many scientists believe that the journey to the Earth could only be made of iron, but it would be too heavy to fly. Plus, the violent cloud storms will make navigation challenging for any spacecraft, unusually as heavy as iron. Jupiter is precisely 779 million km (484 million miles) from the sun, and it takes about 12 years for it to rotate around the sun in its entirety.

It rotates relatively quickly on its own axis, though so its days are concise at only 9 hours, not that it really matters as its very dense cloud cover prevents the planet from penetrating sunlight. Its axial tilt is only 3.13°, so on Jupiter, there are no seasons. Since Jupiter has a magnetic field, the geomagnetic dynamo process is believed to take place at its centre.

This gives scientists a reason to believe that the core of Jupiter is much like ours, but it consists of different elements like hydrogen (75% by mass) and helium (24% by weight), more similar to the sun than the earth. It is also speculated that within the planet itself there is no rocky layer, but a world made up primarily of gasses. The atmosphere of Jupiter spans an altitude of 4,828 km (3,000 miles), the largest in the solar system.

It consists majorly of helium and hydrogen, just like our sun, giving scientists the idea that in early history Jupiter might have developed into a second sun, but did not make the process altogether. Its chemical composition, together with its size and gravitational pull, leads scientists to believe this idea. In a sense, many are referring to Jupiter, and within our solar system, there are many moons and satellites a mini solar system.

The atmosphere is covered thickly in swirling clouds and winds, one of which produces the broad red "chin" noticeable in the planet's equator's southern region of 20°. This great storm is a backward cyclone that swirls eastward while travelling west around the planet. Essentially, Jupiter is covered in major super storms that, if it were to happen here, would eliminate all life on Earth.

Winds reaching nearly 644 km (400 mph), while winds barely reach 322 km (200 mph) on Earth, even in the worst hurricanes. Interestingly, the storm clouds of Jupiter are also moving in opposite directions in bands. No in-depth explanation has been given as to why this happens but observing the planet you can see distinctive lines of clouds that circle the planet, one going west while the next goes east and so on. Violent wind and waves are also not the only things that scare the atmosphere of Jupiter.

Unlike Venus, the atmosphere of Jupiter is packed with radioactive gasses, mainly hydrogen and helium, tearing through the clouds with powerful lighting. Each strike moves at about 274 km (170 miles) per second, much faster than on Earth. The location of Jupiter places it at a distance from which very little of its heat comes from the sun. Temperatures in the upper atmosphere hit just-145 ° C (-234 ° F).

However, as you move closer to the core of the planet, temperatures start to rise to an incredible 24,000° C (43,000° F), much hotter than the sun's surface at just 5,505° C (9,941° F). All the information collated the idea that Jupiter might have been on his way to becoming a second sun, but it ended up somewhere along the process and instead became a gas giant, which is Earth's lucky. By becoming a gas giant, Jupiter has become a shielding Planet since pulling and repelling even dangerous objects away from the earth with its strong gravitational pull. It symbolizes wisdom, restraint, and generosity. Jupiter reveals how we support each other.

Jupiter became a gas giant and has become a bright world since its strong gravitational force draws many dangerous objects out from the earth. Because it always looks ahead, when reading and knowing astrology Jupiter is also aligned with creativity and profession. It is strongly believed that Jupiter has no surface area but is comprised mainly of pure gasses. Most especially helium and hydrogen.

The Juno orbital probe, due to arrive in orbit around Jupiter on July 4, 2016, will in fact provide more knowledge about this. In all, Jupiter comprises 67 recognized satellites and moons orbiting the planet. These objects are grouped into "Jovian Satellites" family groups. The 4 main satellites around Jupiter are called the Galilean Moons.

SATURN

Saturn is our solar system's second biggest; the Earth's sixth planet is another gas giant, while Jupiter is the second largest moon. Saturn's oldest recorded discovery goes back to the ancient Assyrians in 700 BCE, but it is known long before that. It is somewhat less dense than water at 750 times the size of Earth. It is believed that it would float if Saturn were to be thrown into space. This may be because the planet is just a ball of helium, hydrogen, and ammonia, and lacks a stable surface area. Saturn is from the earth 1.4 billion kilometres (886 million miles). It has a broad elliptical orbit that requires 29 years to complete, but only 10.7 hours a day in the rotation on its axis (at a tilt of 26.73 °).

It is believed that the interior of Saturn is similar to that of Jupiter in that it can have a core of iron, nickel and rock composed of silicon and oxygen compounds surrounded by a layer of metallic hydrogen and a combined liquid layer of hydrogen and helium. There would be no active layer but a gaseous surface area consisting of helium and hydrogen that reaches into its upper atmosphere. The environment of Saturn is made up of helium and hydrogen with ammonia crystals in the uppermost part of the atmosphere. Violent storms with wind speeds of more than 160 km (100 mph) rage around the planet with lightning much stronger than those seen on Earth.

Another such storm in its southern polar region travelled a gap equivalent to 2/3 Earth's dimension, which would be from New York to Baghdad. It had an eye for concrete walls close to the Planet hurricanes. This eye produced a vortex or "void" that allowed researchers to see the clouds more than ever before on the Earth. The gravity is lower than on Earth as you descend into Saturn.

A human 68 kg (150 lbs) would weigh only 62 kg (137 lbs) on Saturn, but the pressure on the planet is so high that even a metal spacecraft would crash within a few miles of the upper atmosphere. Saturn has a record of 7 satellites, 46 asteroids, and 9 provisional planets that the planet's orbit has yet to be completely established.

Of these bodies orbiting Saturn, the two most studied are the Titan satellites, which are presumed to have all the infrastructure to create and maintain life, and Enceladus, who has functioning geysers on the surface. Saturn is the planet of constraint and restraint and gives the word saturnine its name. It reveals our sense of discipline, responsibility, focus and personal strength. This includes tenacity, patience, self-control and focus. Saturn can be a positive energy for people to achieve their goals if it is used and directed. Due to its distance from the sun's heat, this gaseous giant remains cold in its upper layers at approximately-178 ° C (-288° F) to -113 ° C (-170° F).

However, in the second layer temperatures change to a range of-88° C (-127° F) to-3° C (-26° F) because of the layer of water-ice. Further down, where heat is generated on the planets, temperatures can range from 57 ° C (134° F) with pressures equal to approximately the same as deep in the oceans of the Earth.

URANUS

This is a unique Planet. For this bazaar Earth, there are two pronunciations, but the most widely used in the scientific world is Ur-uh-nus, but the common way it is said outside of the scientific community is Ur-a-nus. In any event, the name comes from the Greek lord of the Ouranos sky. In 128 BC, astronomer Hipparchos recorded early findings of Uranus, but he thought it was a star.

On March 13, 1781, William Herschel discovered Uranus through a telescope and mistook it for a meteor intending to call it Georgian Sidus after King George III. It was not for months later that Uranus was confirmed by the scientific community to be a planet and not a comet and was called Uranus. Thanks to its size, Uranus was little studied except through near-Earth telescopes and a single study, Voyager 2, as it passed past. It is unremarkable other than horizontally compared to other stars, and it rotates backwards.

This Planet is about 3 billion kilometres from the sun (1.89 billion miles), and it rotates on an intense axial tilt of 97.77° and one day is just 17 hours on Uranus. Still, it takes the world 84 years to complete a revolution around the sun at 6.83 kilometres per second orbital speed. One odd aspect of Uranus is that it happens every 42 years that only one of its poles sees the sun at a time.

Another anomaly is that it not only rotates backwards, west to east but on its side is also the Planet. The poles seem to be on the Planet's eastern and western coasts, and the Earth is moving from north to south. One hypothesis about this anomaly is that, during its ancient past, a large object collided with Uranus' and tilted it to its face. There is no evidence to backing up this hypothesis, though, and there are too many factors to make this explanation impossible.

So, this is a question that can never really be answered until we can finally visit and study the planet. The Uranus density is 14.5 times the Mercury mass and 4 times the Moon mass. Scientists think that its core consists of a rock (silicate and iron-nickel), but that it doesn't have a solid surface under the clouds of its atmosphere, but instead descends into a deep, thick liquid icy mantle.

The pressures become so intense, 800 GPa (Earth's only 364 GPa), that diamonds surround the core of the planet is strongly believed. Like all the other giants of carbon in the solar system, the atmosphere of Uranus consists mainly of gaseous hydrogen and helium. Its soft blue hue derives from the upper atmosphere of 2 per cent methane. Scientists were disappointed when they first observed Uranus, as all they saw was an inactive planet.

Nevertheless, a very active world with violent storms has been discovered on closer measurements, and it turned out that Uranus is the coldest planet in the solar system, much colder than Neptune. Uranus currently has five major satellites, thirteen inner moons and nine irregular moons.

Despite their orbits come extremely close to meeting, they move in a chaotic pattern around Uranus. We are thought to cross paths and clash with each other over time, but this is not going to happen for another 100 million years.

Miranda is one of its most impressive spacecraft. Heavily ravaged with grooves and broken terrain, with a highly unexplained orbital plane that has yet to be understood. Uranus is a revolutionary and regenerating world.

It is pushing fresh ideas and concepts and drawing out the highest potential for men. It is an act of originality, diversity and imagination. It also provides a moral viewpoint and a curiosity in spiritual practices.

NEPTUNE

This is the furthest planet from the sun in the solar system. It is the fourth biggest planet in our solar system with a diameter of 24,621 km (15,299 miles) and the coldest and hottest planet in the world, both physically. Neptune's discovery came from an observation in Uranus orbit's oddity. It did not fit with the law of Newton, so astronomers predicted that beyond Uranus, there would have to be another planet. Two scientists John Couch Adams and Urbain Le Verrier determined the possible position of the supposed 8th planet, but neither wanted to find it on the moon.

Two researchers, Johann Gottfried Galle and Heinrich Louis d'Arrest decided to take a look on September 23, 1846, and Neptune was spotted. Though, two centuries before that, Galileo was the first to see Neptune in reality. He thought, though, that it was a star and did not realize that it was, in fact, a planet, so the observation did not give him recognition. This Planet is 4.5 billion kilometres from the sun (2.8 billion miles). It has an orbit for it to make one rotation around the sun takes 165 years.

Averagely, it takes 16 hours to complete its orbit at 28.32° axial tilt. His days are relatively short while his years are very long. However, it doesn't get much heat from it because of its extreme distance from the sun. Because it is too far away and too expensive to send missions to study the planet further, a lot is not known about this gas giant.

What information is available mainly from the data of Voyager 2 during its flyby and our near-Earth telescopes. It is suggested that molten rock, liquid ammonia, and methane are the inner two-thirds of its inner structure. Within this segment of the planet, a conductive material (most likely water) creates the planets ' oddly-oriented magnetic field with a high tilt of 47 °.

It consists of gasses heated by the core region of the planet in its outer third as it most possibly does not have a hardened crust but an icy mantle in its place. Neptune governs our innermost feelings, our mental abilities, our intelligence, and our creativity. The positive qualities are receptivity, empathy, spiritual growth, intuitive vision, and sympathy. This shows morality and moral values.

CHAPTER SEVEN:
Chart Patterns (Birth Charts)

How does this method of understanding the planet's positions and movements work? What is the concept of a zodiac sign, and how do the planets influence the signs? Such questions are essential for learning the basics of reading the birth charts, showing the positions of the planets in the sky at the time of birth. An analysis of this chart, also known as a natal chart, can provide profound insight into your personality, motivations, and desires. Let's look at how the art of astrology and the ability to read birth charts have evolved, and how you can apply it too. What do the stars have to do with astrology? Since the dawn of time, men have stargazed. Our prehistoric ancestors have tracked impressive phenomena such as eclipses and short-range comets and frequent cyclic patterns over thousands of years.

Distinctive clusters of twinkling stars were considered "constellations," while solid celestial bodies were identified as "planets." Under the calm of the velvety night sky, the moon, Mercury, Venus, Mars, Jupiter, and Saturn — known as the "classical planets "— were found. When you divide the sky into twelve sections, each named after the largest constellation it contained, the ancient Babylonians created the zodiac. The

Zodiac calendar also monitored time and made predictions: The Babylonians noted that celestial passage, or transits, corresponded with both propitious occurrences and natural misfortunes.

At the beginning of the first century, the Romans introduced the zodiac, extending the positions of stars and planets through mythology. Astrology was born at that crossroads of careful study and epic folklore. Astrology has been at the centre of science, medicine, philosophy, and magic for centuries. The "as above, so below" Hermetic axiom means the assumption that the universe's vast, enigmatic macrocosm represents the microcosm of interactions of humans.

The astronomical mystery was solved by the invention of the telescope and the subsequent observation of the so-called "inner planets" — Uranus, Neptune, and Pluto. Although the function of astrology has changed (it is now used to gage romantic compatibility more frequently than to predict the harvest's fate), today we still observe the planets as did the ancient Babylonians.

What are the names of the planets? Astrology is a large, complex and highly specialized science, the basic principles are straightforward: at the moment of your birth, a birth chart is a glimpse of the sky (you can measure yours here). This indicates the exact location of each of the planets and their formation. The Nine Planets are in the same constellation in some birth charts; in others, they are spread across the sky.

As each has its celestial function, the distance between these planets is necessary. Let's glance at every big object in the world. SUN If someone tells you what your sign is, whether they know it or not, they question you about the Sun's location at conception. Our essential meaning is symbolized by the light.

This vibrant heavenly body represents our ego, self-awareness, basic personality, and general preferences. (You can learn more about what the sun sign means about you right here.) The zodiac sign Leo is regulated by the Sun, a vibrant, energetic fire sign that exudes both courage and theatricality. It takes about a month to pass a zodiac sign— or travel across it.

MOON

The moon's gravitational pull controls the oceanic tides and atmosphere. In astrology, the moon is our inner world of emotions. Although the light reveals our outer world, the moon symbolizes everything below the horizon. It represents our most private self's spiritual retreat. The moon governs the Cancer zodiac sign, the sensitive, protective sign of water that defines nutrition, comfort, and safety.

The fastest-moving celestial body; which is the moon, takes around two and a half days to pass through a symbol of the zodiac. The Moon represents fertility and is associated with sensitivity, imagination, feelings, emotions, sub consciousness, and intuition. It also has to do with nursing, housekeeping, and family and home life. Individuals governed by the Moon are primarily emotional, sensitive, and changeable. In advanced and fundamental astrology, the Moon is related to the subconscious mind.

MERCURY; the solar system's thinnest and deepest Planet, is modelled after the Roman goddess who served the gods as a messenger. Mercury symbolizes contact within astrology. Mercury reflects logic and rationality, while the moon reflects our emotions. Mercury is using its clever intellect and unremitting curiosity to analyse, sort, and classify, helping us to synthesize and articulate complex ideas.

Mercury governs the air sign of the Gemini and the earth sign of the Virgo, each of which represents a different aspect of Mercury's expression: Gemini is an exit while Virgo is a source. Mercury transits a zodiac sign for 13 to 14 days and retrogrades three to four times a year. Mercury rules the intellect and the nervous system. It is about self-expression and about getting along with others. Mercury's keyword is communication, which is why it has to do with quick thinking, adaptability, eloquence, sharp perceptions, and intellect. It is also travel related VENUS the Planet; Venus after the enchanting goddess of Rome, Venus is the vibrant planet representing beauty, love, and money. Known in traditional astrology as a "benefic."

Venus has a positive impact (Jupiter is the other advantageous one). The indulgent Venus is best in its lavish form: exquisite foods, prolonged baths and floral hydrating agents resonate with Venus nature. The high-brow tastes of Venus reflect our interest in art and culture, while our idealized perception of love is revealed by its romantic sensibilities. Both Taurus earth sign and Libra air sign are governed by Venus, each representing a different side of the expression of Venus: Taurus is physical, and Libra is cerebral. Venus transits a zodiac sign for about four to five weeks and retrogrades every 18 months. Venus is Love and Sexuality goddess and it also stands for gentleness, sociability, beauty, and arts.

It controls human emotions that are deeper and finer, such as appreciation, love and devotion. Venus reveals what you enjoy and how close relationships are handled. The surface of the planet is but a small part of the problem with Venus when it comes to the possible existence of life there. The atmosphere of Venus is both poisonous, and dense. With 96 per cent carbon dioxide (CO2) and small nitrogen traces, it is so dense that rainfall and lighting occur only in the upper atmosphere.

Which could be a good thing to see as how sulphuric acid rains. Covered in clouds similar to Earth, consisting only of sulphur dioxide, these cloud densities work for the planet in three ways; One, it doesn't allow the light of the sun to reach the surface fully, and so the surface of the planet remains in constant shadow. A larger portion of sunlight reflects off the clouds, which is why Venus appears so luminous in the sky.

Two, it traps the heat on the surface together with the density of its atmosphere, preventing it from escaping. Three, it behaves like a magnetic field, because Venus does not have one. Without this continuously dense cloud layer and dense atmosphere, Venus will probably be much more like Mercury than Earth Essentially a planet which is dead.

The rationale behind the elevated CO2 rates and the sulphuric acid clouds lies under what is on the Earth filled with a massive volcano. These volcanoes emit carbon dioxide and other gasses that are produced from Venus' initial environment. In time, the build-up of these gasses without any way to combat them produced a greenhouse effect that eventually killed Venus ' chances of developing existence.

The surface temperatures on Venus has attained a staggering 467 ° C (872 ° F) and there is no way for the heat to escape the planet due to greenhouse gasses, so there is no difference in temperature between day and night which makes Venus the hottest planet in the solar system. Jointly, the USSR and the USA had 26 missions to Venus. Most of those sent to land on its surface were either crushed or only able to send back minutes of data due to pressures within the planet.

One lander, Venera 14, sent by the U.S.S.R. in 1981, succeeded in landing on the moon and providing both colour and black and white panoramic photographs of the outer planets as well as soil research. Potential flights to Venus were scheduled, but for these projects there are no concrete proposals. MARS is the Red Planet and it is known for its cries of war. Named after the Roman war god, Mars stands for action, determination, and aggression.

His competitive energy also emerges as we struggle to meet a deadline, sprint to catch a flight or fight for a specific spot. Mars is the fire beneath our ass, which provides the energy boost charged with adrenaline that fuels movement. It also represents our love and desire for the flesh. The indiscriminating sign filled with fire; Aries, known for its high octane vivacity, is ruled by this Sun. Mars transits a zodiac sign for about six to seven weeks and retrogrades every two years.

JUPITER

Jupiter— or Zeus, in Greek mythology — the biggest planet in the solar system is recognized for its large presence. In traditional astrology, Jupiter referred to as the "Great Benefit," symbolizes fortune, philosophy, abundance, and spirituality. Our compassionate world controls growth, allowing us to expand our horizon through religion, culture, and schooling. Jupiter governs Sagittarius, known for his thrill-seeking disposition, the adventurous fire sign.

Jupiter transits a Zodiac sign for about 12 to 13 months and goes retrograde for about 120 days each year.

SATURN

Space, laws, and constraints are synonymous with the ringed gas giant. Saturn symbolizes hard work, professional performance, and steadfast resilience on a good day. But, on a miserable day, Saturn can be cruel and painful, pushing us to develop from hard love and demanding obstacles. Although this planet shows its affection in a strange way, Saturn has our best interest in mind. It just wants us to play through the rules. The enterprising Earth sign; Capricorn, known for its tireless ambition, is governed by Saturn, and it takes about two and a half years to pass each sign. It goes backwards for about 140 days each year.

URANUS

Is an unusual planet and also the first planet to be found by a telescope, the only celestial object called after a Greek god and is so turned on its axis that it orbits the sun on its side practically. Uranus is a suitable emblem of science, resistance, and creativity. This progressive world rejects the laws and is always eager to promote complex creative reform. Uranus can have amazing effects (the world likes the benefit of the shock after all). It governs Aquarius, recognized as the free-thinking air sign for its eccentricity and non-conformity. Uranus transits each sign for about seven years and goes retrograde for about 150 days each year.

NEPTUNE

The vivid azure colour of Neptune perfectly complements its astrological meaning. Neptune governs the spiritual unknown's magical, mysterious vastness and importantly, its name was gotten from the Roman God of the Sea.

Immediately a thick fog rolls across the ocean, the separation between the water and the sky is hard to discern. Likewise, at the convergence between fantasy and reality, there is the influence of Neptune. Neptune's energy is highly creative and powerfully psychic on a good day. Neptune, however, can become paranoid and escapist on a poor day. Use the creativity when Neptune's power is felt but note to put an anchor down: You never want to get lost at sea. Neptune governs Pisces, recognized for his incredible imagination and psychic powers as the intuitive water sign. The planet transits each sign for approximately 14 years and retrogrades every year for about 150 days.

PLUTO

Pluto; this frozen celestial body, by astrological means, did not measure up to the scientific concept of a planet, Pluto is still a big deal.

Pluto symbolizes strength, transformation, destruction, and regeneration. Pluto's power has its roots in the darkness, named after the underworld Roman God ("Hades"). This beguiling planet slithers seamlessly into complex infrastructures, transforming systems quietly from within.

Pluto reminds us that we must release the past in order to manifest change. It is synonymous with Scorpio, the enigmatic sign of water characterized by its mystical structure. Pluto transits each sign for approximately 14 to 30 years and retrogrades every year for about 185 days. In basic astrology, Pluto, the ruler of the sub world, represents the subconscious. It shows the capacity to change, to rebuild, to evolve, to recover and to learn.

Because, Pluto takes 250 years for the zodiac to be completed, the effect of Pluto is having an impact on the generations of the population and can change world conditions. The importance of the outer planets in a birth chart relies on their residences. There will be twelve parts of a birth chart known as the houses.

It takes care of six address everyday activities and worldly issues such as personal finances, households and routines; households. Seven through 12 deal with more abstract concepts, including philosophy, legacy and psychological skills. The placing of the planets in the houses shows where we store our energy and our strengths and our weaknesses. Find the planets and their accompanying signs and houses and study your chart.

How is the work of a Planet determined by its zodiac sign, and which area of life has the most direct impact on it? Your distinctive interpretation of a birth chart should go through this formula: Planet + Sign + House = Interpretation from here onwards. For instance, if your birth moon in the seventh house is delicate to cancer, the house that reflects dedicated relationships, your emotional satisfaction may be very linked with you.

If in the 11th House, the House associated with humanitarianism, your natal Mars is in pragmatic Virgo, you may be motivated to help others in efficient ways. Your rising sign, also recognized as your ascendant, defines the unique placement of planets in buildings. This is the zodiac symbol that was at the exact moment of your conception on the eastern horizon.

The rising sign determines the whole design of your birth chart which identifies the monarch of your celestial system, the planet aligned with your chart (to measure yours, find your rising sign and then which planet rules your zodiac sign). This rising sign often determines our outward experience. If the speech is composed by your sun sign; how the statement is produced is your rising sign.

Astrologers describe this as "the mask worn in public." This shows how others view you and how you communicate with the universe. Whether you are a professional astrologer or just making sense of your birth chart, understanding the planets, signs, and houses can expose astrological wisdom's complex depths. Spend a lot of time with your birth chart: when you relate the chart to your everyday life, the capacity to perceive the placements in it will be improved. Don't worry about creating narratives and making bold remarks.

That's how the solar system was created after all. The universal conviction that the human spirit represents the cosmos is at the core of astrology, the celestial knight: both are uniquely complex and profoundly enigmatic. And in the centre, the practice of stargazing is astrology. The silence will always be illuminated by the curiosities.

Aspects

In a horoscope, the positions between the various planets are considered aspects. They are another important concept for understanding basic astrology and can reinforce, weaken and affect each planet's readings. There are both positive and unfavourable aspects to this. A planet can often be favourable to one or more planets and at the same time be unfavourable to others. Ironically, individuals use different aspects of theirs.

One person could suffer immensely under the effects of a discordant aspect, while another with the exact same aspect will look for and work with the positive energies within the aspect.

Favourable Aspects

The beneficial implications illustrate the worlds' optimistic, helpful forces. We show the areas of life where you can do with little effort what you set out to do. That is why a lot of people take them for granted and become lazy. It is important to work as diligently in these fields as anywhere else to optimize the blessings you have got.

The favourites are:

Conjunction: This happens when two planets fall within eight degrees of each other. Usually the conjunctions indicate areas that will deliver good results.

Trine: It arises when the planets are about 120 degrees apart, with an 8-degree leeway on either hand. The trine is the luckiest element, since the two planets' forces readily harmonize.

This feature also tells you where the abilities are most.

Sextile: It occurs when the planets are about 60 degrees apart, with an 8-degree leeway on either hand. This is a "simple" feature that usually works without much feedback from you in your favour.

Semi-sextile: It occurs when the planets are about 30 degrees separated, again with an 8-degree leeway on either hand. This is also an element of "free." But, in your interpretation of astrology, you should not take it for granted as it suggests places in which you can shine.

Unfavourable Aspects

It occurs when the planets are about 30 degrees apart, once again with an 8-degree leeway on either hand. That is also an element of "free." Nevertheless, in your understanding of astrology, you shouldn't take it for granted, as it reveals areas where you can shine.

Opposition: It develops when the two planets are about 180 degrees separated, with an 8-degree leeway on either side. That's a problematic aspect, and it takes a lot of effort to solve the challenges that it produces.

Square: It happens when the two planets are around 90 degrees separated, with an 8-degree leeway on either side. This aspect works against your best interests, and much hard work is needed to eradicate the hostility it creates.

CHAPTER EIGHT:
Connection Between Human Behavior And The Alignment Of The Stars And Planets

We, humans, have a link with the planets and stars around us. The most profound and closest connection we have is with the planets of our own solar system. The location of the planets has had an effect on the body since the creation of humanity. These celestial influences on human conformity create different arrangements which express them.

When an individual is born, the precise location of every planet in the solar system, including the stars, is reflected in the various houses of astrology (Aries, Taurus, Gemini...). This action and configuration influence human life on Earth. These planets have a natural force that affects the individual's biological, physical, mental-emotional states. Their different configurations, locations, and sizes have either positive or negative effects on the human race.

There is a mutual relationship between the influence the planets have on us and how we react. Human beings can feel the forces of change in planetary positions in all of their behaviour. Astrologers can predict how the change can affect us all over the planet, and how people can mitigate their forces by properly implementing principles.

These can assess the attitude by studying a person's birth chart in detail and thus are used as a hypothesis to help explain the aspects of life-based on celestial signs. All of us are magnificent creatures, perfect and intricate. As a result, we need to raise the bar a little bit and give a little more substance to our astrological makeup. Far too many of us are led to believe that we represent ONE particular symbol, referred to as our Sun Sign.

The fact is that, yes, each of us is born with a special stamp that we call our "sign." But it's a combination of more than one piece of the Zodiac. Sun sign or astrological label is just a sign in which the Sun lived when we were born, and every sign links us to others born around the same time of year. Most people born under the same Sun sign share similar values and sometimes have unique ties.

It's like you're part of the same group. The explanation for this recognition of the symbol is all about the movements of the Sun. Throughout the calendar year, the Sun moves through every 12 signs of the Zodiac. What our Sun Symbol was decided by the sign that the sole was at the very moment when we were born. The indication that we were born with the Sun dictated what our Sun Sign would be.

It is like a clock tick with an hour's hand topping, each time the hour's hand hits a new number; the signs are changed. The Sun usually lives for the same period every year in each sign — almost a month. Yet, it doesn't stay exactly the same every year. It may be somewhat difficult to start or end with each sign, as the signs will be changed.

There are people who have gone years thinking that they had a particular zodiac sign, but they were actually wrong. For example, in New York City, someone who was born on 21 December 2020 at 18:00 will have a Sun sign of Sagittarius. If someone else was born the same day and position just 3 minutes later (approximately 18:03 p.m.), the Sun sign was in Capricorn.

The Sun will always be turned into the next sign each year, and the time for this transition into the next sign is not the same every year. If a birthday falls at the end of the start or end of the sign, this person will have the traits of two signs running through him. This is called a "cusp." Zodiac Cusp Zodiac cusps are the twilight days between the signs one ascends as the other sets.

It's a good time to be created — these are periods of transformation, ends and beginnings, compromise and surprise. Each cusp period has a name that mirrors its distinctive energy. · Cusp of Strength: 16 April-22 Energy Cusp: 17 May-23 Magic Cusp:: 17 June – 23 Cusp of Oscillation: 19 July – 25 Cusp of Exposure: 19 August – 25 Cusp of Beauty: 19 September – 25 Cusp of Drama: 19 October – 25 Cusp of Revolution: 18 November – 24 November Cusp of Prophecy: December 18 - 24 Cusp of Mystery: January 16 - 23 Cusp of Sensitivity: February 15 - 21 Cusp of Rebirth: March 17 - 23

You may notice that if you are born on the cusp of your neighbourhood symbol, you have personality traits. People born under Aries for instance, but on the cusp of Aries-Taurus, also make great leaders.

Usually, you could have made quick decisions and responded too quickly if you were an Aries, but if you were an Aries born on the cusp of Taurus, these characteristics could be tempered with a more rooted, responsive Taurean energy. However, this does not mean those born in a cusp would always have it all hulky-dory; the energies of their two signs might collide. Nevertheless, being born on the cusp will offer you a variety of qualities that can combine and shine in various ways.

In the world of astrology, the Cusps are controversial! While cusps are used by some astrologers, most of them are not. A person's astrology diagram is based on specific calculations that show a person's zodiac sign point-blank. But if on the cusp a person is born, and he really feels the effect of two signs.

Here is how that can be clarified. The Sun sign is a key component of the birth chart which represents the overall strength and unique characteristics that a person learns to acquire and communicate effectively during this lifetime. What sign and house the Sun is placed in reveals, with the greatest possible luminosity, how and where you will appear in your life. The idea of sign cusps not only dilutes the value of Sun.

Each sign comprises 30 degrees, adding up to a perfect 360-degree globe. The definition of sign cusps is a misnomer because, although you were born on a day when the Sun changed signs, the mathematics will become apparent. It is difficult to explain your relationship with the sign before or after your Sun sign because you were born on this cusp. Your Sun sign is strong, transparent and luminous: he knows who he should be.

If you believe you are binding to the qualities of your Sun sign's neighbouring sign, this is probably due to the fact that one of the specific planets moving close to the Sun is located in that sign to which you are related. Assuming you were born on the Aries-Taurus cusp, a proper astrology chart for the date, time and location of your birth would clearly show whether your Sun is at the final degree of Aries or the first degree of Taurus.

If you were born when the Sun passed through the final degree of Aries but can refer to the qualities of Taurus, this is most likely due to the fact that Mercury, Venus, Mars, the Moon, or even your Rising sign is in Taurus! We are not just one sign. Of course, just a few can resonate profoundly with their sign's "common" characteristics. Others will say they're "not related in any way" to the generalities. Personalities are always different from all the assumed generalities of the Sun Sign.

For example, many people tend to interpret Leo as an emblem with a dramatic flair which always needs an audience. But sometimes you can meet Leo, who would tell you that he is shy. Or a Capricorn, who is supposed to be known for responsibility, discipline, self-control and good manners. Can tell you that he is an utter anarchist and never abides by the rules?

Since we are all so unique individuals, it is impossible to classify all of us in just twelve different ways. The most important zodiac influence is OUR RISING SIGN. Our Rising Symbol was a symbol that at the very moment we were born was "waking up" or rising. Surprisingly enough, this sign represents us much more than our sign of the Sun.

The -Symbol features paint the façade–and when visitors first come across us, they see those attributes first. Only when they meet us can they see our Sun Sign, and how we choose to shine. Everyone can see our outer shell – but not everybody can see what is on the other side.

Our Rising Symbol, or Ascendant, becomes incredibly powerful as we learn about how our temperament is influenced by the Zodiac. Sometimes the features of that symbol can be much stronger than the Sun sign itself. Take that silent & shy Leo; we talked about earlier. He is actually a Cancer Rising, and he needs to tuck away from the limelight in his shell. Only when he has confidence in his crowd would he let them in. Only then can you see his genuine or vivid creative side of Leo. Also, remember the defiant Capricorn.

He's an Aquarius Rising, and he's displaying a very defiant and peculiar attitude to all he sees. He has goals and aspirations like every Capricorn, but they're not seen in any forms as the "standard." Astrology can be an instrument that sheds a lot of light on who we are and why we work the way we do. It can also show the people that we will actually interact with, as well as those that we will definitely not.

But, if we don't look at the full picture, all of its value is lost. We have to throw away the thought that each person only has one sign. It is time we accepted the idea that we are made up of several signs of the Zodiac and their effects. At the very moment we are born, everything begins, and we take our first breath. That is where our true story starts.

At that moment, the Sun was in a particular position, but there were nine other celestial bodies that had something to say about us as well. Every one of those planets was also residing in a symbol that is vital to our personality: The Sun tells how we glow. Also accountable for the energy levels a person has liveliness and the hearts functioning. The Sun defines our higher-level spirit and our lower-level ego.

This represents who we are inside ourselves. This reveals our true will, life's main purpose, and dream. The Sun governs Leo's sign. This affects the good part of lifestyle that helps us to "shine" through acts, vacations, public actions and different types of games. It's known to be highly vibrant. This influences an individual's imagination, too.

Throughout a season the Sun moves through every indication of astrology and at each sign it uses monthly. Therefore, as the Sun is a star, the birthday of a person is affected by the different sun symptoms in which the Sun lasts on that 30 days. It affects creativity within a person, showing how they experience art, company, children, and being parent-especially fatherhood. On - the-go planet Mercury shows us how we interact.

Mercury governs intellectual, innovative and creative thought, the capacity to make complex equations, and so on. He travels the best of all the stars, the fastest, maintaining the prestige of being named a runner, traveller, and communicator. It takes things apart and then brings them back together to demonstrate their positive attitude, motivation and excitement. Mercury is regarded as a personal planet which represents a person's psychology.

This allows us to better understand human psychology, acting as a link between an individual being and the environment around. Health problems such as thyroid problems, brain problems, respiratory problems and the nervous system problems are linked to mercury. The element of mercury is water in Chinese astrology. It is therefore diplomatic, friendly and very intuitive. Mercury is called Buddha in Hindu astrology, or better as Buddhi, indicating wisdom and correspondence.

People under Mercury's influence are very clever. The lovely Venus, or loving planet, shows where our heart lies and where we might get some mutual support. The salient representation of relationship and harmony. Venus is a fast-moving personal planet reflecting man's daily mind and the woman he loves.

Venus influences our attitudes to society, modesty, morality, honesty, grace, joy and well-being, sense of beauty, love and peace, encourages people to socialize and make friends. Venus also focuses heavily on relationships with the genders. Venus resembles mercury more or less. They're still three months in their life cycles. Nevertheless, the energy of Venus is more than that of mercury. It rules over the passion and happy sense of beauty.

There is a strong connection between the world and romance as it regulates the hormone estrogen. It is known as the society's building block because it encourages people to socialize and work together as one. It's difficult for a solid, independent Venus to find another of the same character. Earth, the world suffering, says how we are going to fight and stand up for you. Mars exhibits the mindset of an individual.

The brilliant red shade reflects a torrent of blood, energy, movement and attraction. Mars is Aries' leading authority shaping and producing, Scorpio influencing power and libido and Capricorn affecting ambitions and dedication. Mars, being the dominant factor, is particularly passionate and aggressive, reflecting nature, self-discipline, will strength, and stamina.

Mars has a powerful influence on your libido, your curiosity and your sexuality. This helps us to live up to our ambitions. They help us get involved in our goals making their influence important as they are able to figure out how we engage and achieve our goals in life. Mars helps one to work out the person to launch a scenario and evaluate a prospective lover-from being coolly divided to the enchanting intensity and every style between them. On the ego too, Mars will generate adverse force.

When its strength is used for obvious requirements, it may inflict destruction. Sometimes it erupts slowly, witnessing tantrums without self-control or becoming easily irritated by a constant. It helps an individual to be guided, and the features of Mars are easily recognized and perfected. People influenced by Mars are excellent in operation, competition, industry, and management.

Mars guides the parts of the sex body, the kidney and the muscle system, the feeling of flavour, face, remaining ear, renal system, inflamed circumstances, uses up, injuries and intimately transmitted diseases to your health. Jupiter, or the zodiac symbol Santa Claus, shows where we have a remarkable element of excess. It's the world of growth and grace. It is always geared at divine wisdom, imagination, opportunity, moral knowledge, and the Holy Spirit.

It's also related to an individual's good fortune, wealth, development and extension. Jupiter rules the inner sense of justice and morality within a person. Jupiter is commonly associated with liberty, creativity, and joviality. Exerts a great influence over man's physical, mental, emotional, economic and materialistic existence. It represents success, progress, wealth, employment, and popularity.

Jupiter is one of the favoured stars because it symbolizes success, positive existence, development in mind and spirit. Inside the astrological charts, Jupiter is known to be a societal planet that does not affect the makeup of personality but is of a social nature. It contains the best of what life holds for us.

Best qualities of Jupiter are seen as good humour, good faith, and compassion, but they can be viewed negatively because of blind optimism, greed, irresponsibility, and overindulgence. This reflects the way we show our kindness and compassion. education, and regulating muscular development, joints.

Saturn is synonymous with the principles of restriction, limits, limitations, flexibility and reality, crystallization, and Saturn is considered to be the last part of the actual universe, marking a significant gap in the time series of the trans-Saturnine system and its symptom duration. Saturn has seven rings representing that man has certain limitations, constraints, and delays. Saturn gives us all our education and also teaches us what is right and wrong in life.

Obstacles, mistakes, setbacks and uncertainties show us how to function the right way. Their goals, inspiration, profession, leadership are controlled by the world and affect their own sense of duty, commitment and discipline. It also reflects the interpersonal ability of an individual and how to overcome hardships. Offers hard work and professionalism, and the ability to pressurize. Saturn is more professional and career-based.

Individuals affected by Saturn tend to push into job areas such as corporate management, management, schooling, design, governmental function, industry, oppressive roles, and self-employment. Provides hard work and discipline, and the power to pressurize. Saturn's more professional and career-based. Individuals affected by Saturn tend to push into job areas such as corporate management, management, schooling, design, legislative function, industry, hierarchical roles, and self-employment.

Saturn's acts were looked upon with fear and bad omen. Saturn is a balancing planet though now. It poses tough work and achievement for a guy. Saturn affects circulation, constipation, vitamin deficiency, hearing sensitivity and our teeth. Uranus, the great soul-shaker and awakener, reveals that every one of us is special, defiant and cutting edge. Uranus describes an individual's nervous system. It is 1,782 million miles away from the Earth.

Uranus carries in us improved and more analytical and emotional faculties. Individuals who are influences under Uranus are either destructive in nature, or they work towards natural progress. Uranus' entire cycle lasts 84 years-the same as one period of human life. Can control transition–any kind of change of mind, some drastic and unforeseen shift.

Since Uranus has been attributed to these values, Uranus is associated with any type of change or reformation. It is called a trans-personal planet as it is one of the three outer planets between Neptune and Pluto. Like Neptune and Pluto whose orbits are much longer, several people experience Uranus moving to his previous position in advance of time.

We experience the change from puberty to maturity when we are 21 years old, a period when obligations and the increasing roles of family life are forced on us. "mid-life crisis" is linked to Uranus' half-circuit at age 42. And many of us at the age of 63 consider stopping working and take life retirement. We can find a Uranus co-relationship on us here. The vast majority of humanity may not see Uranus' full return; nevertheless, the same may be witnessed by some who are fortunate.

Neptune's position is special and supersedes all material ties. Most myths and healers are inspired by this world. Neptune's negative effects may confuse an individual who has not yet attained the promised spirituality. This impels other people to explore and indeed strive to feel the influence of Neptune by things like drugs and other mind-altering substances since it is one's inherent existence.

This has to be thought into as the materialization cycle from the point of view of the human soul's development. The happiness of helping a fellow human being, a relative, and a neighbour gives us great satisfaction and makes us break our ego. In this way, a person will lower his restricted ego, and through these actions enjoy the everlasting nature of love. Here is where Neptune steps through.

Realm of Neptune's action is both the perception and the transcendence of the illusion which we call life and universe. There is a legend about a cord that appears to a drunkard as a serpent. There's no real snake. It just seems to happen. Another effective example; you can remove a thorn lodged in your thigh with another thorn. And after this, you get rid of the thorns.

Neptune's behaviour is like the thorn in this sense-it's interdependent. We have to use that delusion to interpret it as deception, and eventually overcome the illusion. Neptune, the creative planet that can get us in, shows in which area of our lives we may get lost. Pluto, the planet which scientists say is not really important enough to be classified as such, reveals where our life will be most transformed.

Astrologically, Pluto is named the "Great Renewer" and is thought to be a part of the human who kills in order to be replaced. Reflects more basic aspects of human development such as motivation and it also describes reduction and change. Individuals under Pluto's control prefer to use authority ruthlessly in their negative way. It symbolizes death and regeneration. It also symbolizes the corrosion of the old and the start of the new.

It is an evolutionary process where all living beings die after a lifestyle phase is over, and a new factor emerges in place. Pluto completes a complete cycle in 248 years and can live between 15 and 20 years in a sign that indicates there are development and conception number of times in its life cycle. Observers, Pluto has a tangible and lasting impact on us.

The Moon reveals how we are when we are most down and where we run. It is said to indicate the feelings of sorrow, happiness, and emotion; it is connected with the sentiments and reminiscences of the soul, their conscious and unconscious thinking, and their ideas. It is also correlated with motherhood, maternal instincts or promotes growth, properties, need for security and past times, especially early encounters and years of childhood.

The Moon has an impact on the nature of the planet, which helps in the ebb and flow of tides. The Moon orbits the Earth 28 days, each of which is agreed for 2.33 years. The Moon has four different stages. Many rewarded in the first stage (1-7.5 days) are fine, excited about Aries taking over their characteristics. We are optimistic in nature and very jovial. They appreciate the relationship and make the first effort and find attention in new types of projects. They have a powerful drive and motivation and are always lifestyle successful.

Again, those born in the first one fourth are generally a bit self-centred and over-sensitive from the adverse factor. In the second stage (7.5 -15 days), blessed individuals are very serious and enjoy a superb position. Most Cancer's and Leo's symptoms manage their features highly. They always want to be in the spotlight. Even if they don't get upset easily, managing them is challenging if they do. They have a greater sense of respect and partnerships with importance. They have a charming personality. Third-stage individuals (15-22.5 days) are delicate and psychological.

Libra and Scorpio also have an impact on them. They stick to their intuitions and are very careful. They're inclined to get drawn to those who are very effective. They love friends and contacts; they are typically strict and insecure; however, they find successes in lifestyle because of their great values.

Those who are blessed in one-fourth (22.5-29 days) are just like the symptoms of Capricorn and Pisces. They are slowly gardeners, but later in their lives, they discover individual and extraordinary accomplishments. They are likely to find themselves a little more nervous, being oversensitive and irritated by other people's requirements. They do not stick to reasoning. The Moon has a more powerful effect than the light for many people who are born under the water signs Mercury, Scorpio and Pisces.

It represents personal needs, and if happiness is needed in life, it is very necessary to keep a balance with the Moon. The Moon can influence our imagination, intuition, and allow us to be sentimental, adaptable, and protective, but it can also cause agitation, irrationality, and mood. With these, you can see that there are actually connections between human behaviour and the alignment of the stars, and you can also see some effects that it has on us.

CHAPTER NINE:
Toolbox For Astronomy

Having talked about how human behaviours relate to the alignment of the star and the planet, let's move to the toolkit in astrology.

There are certain things in your quest for astrology that you'd need to keep in check, which I call "The Toolbox." You'd have to understand every bit of this part; I'd try my best to break it down into short forms. The toolboxes are; the Chart Wheel than the Astrological Houses and the House Cusps and finally the Planets.

A chart wheel

You are going to need a copy of a new chart, preferably your version. A circular diagram divided into twelve equal pieces should be the chart; it should almost look like a family pizza; each piece should be 30 degrees. Every part of the map should have an extension. Every slice of pizza will indicate the Twelve Astrological Houses; a room allocated to each section of the table. We have planet symbols in different houses with their astrological signs, degrees, and minutes of position within that sign.

The twelve house cusps represent each part of the extension, you should have known the signs of the zodiac at this junction, but there are 12 signs of the planet: Sagittarius, Capricorn, Aquarius, Pisces, Aries, Taurus, Gemini, Cancer, Leo, Virgo, Libra and Scorpio. Some of these Zodiac signs may be somewhat similar; you can check their signs on the internet because you need to be able to identify each zodiac sign strictly without mixing them up.

You would also need to test the Planets and the Angles, even though the Planets have a two angle division; the Sun, Planets. The Sun and the Moon are in the party of Lights. The nine planets we have except the Moon, Mercury, Venus, Earth, Mars, Jupiter, Saturn, Uranus, Neptune, and Pluto with two symbols and then the angles of the Lunar Nodes are Ascendant and Midheaven.

Follow me closely on the chart; identify 270 degrees that should be on the 9th when compared to an analogue wall clock, number the pie itself and not the line dividers count in the clockwise direction, count straight until you're back on the 270. You will be numbering your pies from 1 to 12. Now considering the line dividers, assign the Zodiac signs in the same way (counter-clockwise) from the 9th hour in the same order above, contrasting the map with the same clock.

As you can see, this house cusp is in the zodiac sign of Virgo Indeed, as the chart wheel shows, the 10th house cusp starts at 25 degrees and 21 minutes from the Virgo zodiac sign and goes to 18 degrees and 32 minutes into the Libra Zodiac sign, which marks the end of the 10th House and the beginning of the 11th House (the cusp). House cusps accompany each other along with the Zodiac's normal (counter-clockwise) motion, as it appears in the circle of the map.

We have now drawn the wheel of the map and the twelve cusps of the room. For instance, the Sun was in Cancer's Zodiac sign at 25 degrees and 48 minutes at my birth. By looking at my birth chart, we can see that the cusp of the 8th House begins at 15 degrees of Cancer and ends at 25 degrees of Leo. My Moon, therefore, sits within the 8th House at 25 degrees of Cancer and can be pencilled in.

If you've got a computer program, it's all done for you. The growing planet is placed in an appropriate room. When, as is often the case, there is more than one planet in a house, and then each planet in that House is put in the usual Zodiac order.

In this chart, we have the Sun, Pluto, and Venus in the 8th House. These three are put in the 8th chamber, first in the Moon, then in Pluto, and then in Venus, as they are in the zodiac in that order. I hope it's all a bit obvious. The only thing you are expected to understand is the chart wheel's basic circular shape, the twelve house cusps as they occur around the outer edge, and how the planets are placed in the right House. Look at your chart of your own and review these three things.

Different Patterns of Chart Wheels - The Twelve House Standard Wheel Ancient Astrologers, particularly those in India and the Far East, have not even used round chart wheels over the years to this day. Most of the shapes were square. The format explained to you is that the round chart wheel with twelve equally spaced houses was, however, the most popular form used in the 20th century.

Each style of chart has twelve 'equal-size' spaces, although almost no astrological house system, apart from the Equal House system, has houses that are generally 30 degrees in size, but we still use the map wheel because it makes the chart look smooth and offers equal space for writing on the planets in each House. It comes with scalloped quarters, lotus-shaped map rods, and so on in a fancy array.

Interested astrologers in the house system, which more accurately represented the actual space of each room, created a house wheel identical to the regular map globe, except that it displayed the actual space that each House had taken up. Many parts of the Zodiac pie in this House are bigger than others.

The ascending or first cusp of the House is still on the left; however, if you try to imagine that we would have a chart showing the actual amount of space allocated to each House instead of showing all the houses as having 30 degrees of space equivalent. A side benefit of this type of chart is that it is possible to draw a small indicator in the centre of a chart that shows something about the patterns of appearance that make up the chart at a glance.

With uneven houses, this means that the positions of the planet are approximately where they should be on a 360-degree wheel. This would not operate in the traditional wheel of houses, as the planets are spatially limited to the equivalent houses of 30 degrees, and these are only rarely true enough to bring out the patterns. This chart format is still very popular, above.

European astrologers enjoyed seeing the planets drawn in the zodiac circle at the right degree; they didn't like squeezing a bunch of planets into the house systems of equal size. The result has been the so-called Euro Wheel. As you can see, we still have twelve houses, with the ascending or the first house cushion on the far left, but there is more emphasis on the twelve signs— the zodiac band. They even added colour to give each sign a distinct feel.

Here we're using a variant of what's called the Queen's Color Scale. The room in the centre of the chart wheel is ideal in colour to draw a tiny indicator that helps to display the main trends of the chart at a glance. Many variants also display the twelve house numbers. There are many variations in this type of chart, and this is one of the most commonly used chart types today, both here and in Europe.

The "Open Wheel" or "360-Degree Wheel" chart is another very common chart type in use today. Also, this format is a step closer to accentuating the zodiac band. Note it positions the twelve signs in the traditional position, with Aries to the left, Capricorn to the right, and so on, all around. Then, in unequal mode, the twelve houses are drawn where they belong in the zodiac the houses are deemphasized in this style in favour of the zodiac's fixed position in space. This form of chart design is excellent to keep track of everything out there in space, such as the numerous fixed stars, as well as the important points, such as the Galactic Center (G.C.), which is about 26 degrees from Sagittarius.

Rather than having to look through the wheel of the map to see a point like the G.C. This happens; you should look right at 26 degrees of Sagittarius, as it's always there. This style is disadvantageous to the point that you need to figure out where the first cusp of the House is, or any of the other cusps, and this may be frustrating.

But for those astrologers like me who are more interested in the large-scale patterns of the chart and less worried about the house location, the shape of this chart or a variant of it, maybe the chart wheel of choice, leading me to what comes next to the chart shape that I'm actually using. I've been using the Open wheel for years now. Each planet is placed in the Zodiac exactly where it is going or as close to it as possible.

At the centre of the chart, the main aspects are drawn in coloured lines (opposition, trine, square, sextile, etc.) to illustrate the main patterns. Note that the houses are still being deemphasized. Only the ascendant descendant axis (red line) and the Midheaven I.C. are drawn in here. The red arrow marks the ascendant, or cusp of the First House, and the blue arrow marks the Midheaven, or cusp of the Tenth House the colour might be different depending on the chart. The other cusps of the House are not even shown, so you can better understand this if you are interested. My preference for this is because I am more interested in the two axes of the chart than I am in the intermediate cusps.

The intermediate cusps vary depending on which house system you use, and there are now dozens of house systems, but the two axes (Ascendant and Midheaven) are the same for most of the major house systems. In the four major quadrants, my interest is more than in the houses between them.

In addition, when I want to look at the houses separately, I can use a standard wheel of houses, although rarely. In summary, we looked at what are probably the most popular chart wheel formats used by amateur and professional astrologers today but remember that there are literally hundreds of wheel variants out there.

The Twelve Houses

We already know that we have twelve houses and that we connect them with our beliefs, strengths, weaknesses, behaviours, etc. We also know that the twelve houses control twelve aspects of our lives.

First home: The First House is about you, who you are, and how you appear or come across the impact that you have on your first meeting. This reflects the total sum of what you've managed to get together so far in your life and what you can put on the table for all of you to see your whole package. This House deals with the personal aspect of life, including appearances and obvious arrangements.

Second House: The Second House has to do with money and possessions, but also with how you acquire, measure, and love things in life. This marks your willingness (or lack of it) to expand on what you have been given and to turn your ideas and plans into something concrete and powerful. It tests your listening receptivity and capacity and taking things in and using them. The financial aspect of life, such as income, property, value systems, resources, prosperity and stability, is part of this House.

Third House: The third House is about connectivity and collaboration, about how to reach out, discover, and simply network with both people and things your ability to connect. This is the networking house at large; Contact, Messages, Speech, Email, Mobile, Gossip, Connections, Links, Family, Siblings, Discovery, Investigations, Inquiry, Short Trips.

Fourth House: The Fourth House is about the overall life experience you've gained around you and how you feel about life, especially when it comes to home and family issues. This House deals with Home Experience, The Thrill of the Trip, In the

Moment, Safety, Operations Base, The Chariot, Parents, Home, and Roots.

Fifth House: The Fifth House tells us how to express ourselves and how creative we are. This includes our awareness of what we've done, and maybe they're proud of it: all forms of creating whatever we've been able to express and get out of it. I'm referring to anything we've created and of course to our children.

Also: to teach and show what we have learned or know about others. This House deals with the imaginative aspects of life, such as speech, children, artistic works, trust, culture, ego.

Sixth House: The Sixth House is said to be the House of Health, but it is broader than that, how we take care of ourselves. The House also applies to how we care; not only about our own person but also about how we care about others and issues that need our attention and care. Keep in Mind thorough care and attention. This House deals with the health aspects of life, such as nutrition, preservation, salvation, care, fare, proactive, nursing, stress.

Seventh House: The Seventh House is the position in which we go beyond our personal concerns and take an interest in others, whether it is an interest in the general public or an interest in a specific person with whom we are committed. That's why this House has to do with partnerships, with responsiveness to someone other than ourselves. This House deals with the aspect of the life of marital and other partnerships.

Eighth House: The Eighth House has been said to apply primarily to sex, but this is too small of a description. This House has a lot to do with how we hack through the red tape and get right down to the nitty-gritty, to where things are really at. Here's where we're going to strip away the veneer and get to the bare facts. It has more to do with industry and with an important trade than with sexuality. This House is about sex, death, regeneration, analysis, exchange, criteria.

Ninth House: The Ninth House refers to the ideas and concepts of life that are of the utmost importance to us, those that will endure or last; therefore, this House often tells us something about the kind of spirituality or religion that suits us. In any case, it is here that we can only find the most important parts of our lives, the parts that are most relevant to us. This House is about reality, long journeys, faith, philosophy, law, cleansing.

Tenth House: The Tenth House has to do with our vocation or profession, which is the place of life in which we can see and treat in a natural way. This is where we have an innate vision of taking control and controlling things; in reality, it is our ability to be effective. Profession, status, reputation, vision, oversight, practical talents, vocation, management is what this House is all about.

Eleventh House: The Eleventh House has been called the House of friends, and it is here that we find signs of our ability to work with others and participate in a common dream, a vision of a society or country working together for a cause that is greater than our own personal self-interest. This eleventh house deals with the community aspects of life, such as altruism, groups, aspirations, friends, planning, and sharing.

Twelfth House: The Twelfth House shows that there is a need for versatility and humility, even sacrificing our own personal needs to further a cause greater than ours. This is where we find more acceptances and how we find the means to embrace whatever life presents fully. This House deals with the sacrificial aspects of life, such as confinement, unconsciousness, secrecy, self-defence, patience, and understanding.

House Cusps: The twelve astrological houses divided the zodiac circle into twelve roughly equal pie-shaped houses, and in most cases, each of these twelve houses had one of the signs of the zodiac on the so-called "Cusp." To be precise, the Ascendant is Sagittarius at 8-degrees and 1 minute. The cusp of the Descendant or seventh house is on the far right — at Gemini's8-degree and 1 minute.

At the top of the chart is the 10th house cusp (also called the Midheaven), at 25-degrees and 21 minutes from the Virgo zodiac sign. The opposite position or 4th house cusp (also called the I.C.) is of the zodiac sign Pisces at 25-degrees and 21 minutes. The minutes can be calculated using computers. Planets The planets and their symbols tell their own story, and one worth listening to. I would recommend that you check the online images of the symbols.

1. The Sun: It's relatively simple, combining a point and a circle. The point represents the matter, or the point, and the spirit of the circle.

Or, here is the ultimate symbol of full cycle (circle) expansion and complete contraction. This is the Alpha and the Omega, the one and all.

This concerns our profession or "the way of life" and is an example of our social standing and reputation. The Descendant is the point directly opposite the Ascendant on the birth chart. It is the cusp of the birth chart's seventh House which is one of the chart wheel's corners. The Imum Coeli (I.C.) is the cusp of the birth chart's 4th House one of the corners at the end of the list.

The 12 Zodiac signs we have Let us take the time to go through some of the main astrological symbols and examine some brief comments on them. The 12 signs of the zodiac: Aries, Capricorn, Aquarius, Pisces, Taurus, Gemini, Cancer, Leo, Virgo, Libra, Scorpio and Sagittarius.

Aries Symbol: The soul crescent, upside down, on a single shaft which can be seen either as a sprout or as a device to dig or puncture. It conventionally depicts a Ram's head. Taurus Symbol: The spirit circle, with the soul crescent on top open and receiving; maybe it should look like a Bull, but it is the best symbol for the most receptive Taurus. Gemini symbol: It, of course, actually represents number two—Twins—and a mirror-like image.

Cancer Symbol: The spirit circle and the soul crescent combined, then interfaced with each other. Yes ... Cancer, the Crab, but beyond that — a powerful symbol of being.

Leo Symbol: Now we have the circle of spirit, and along with it, what we can call two forms of the soul's crescent; these are combined to create a structure almost unfolding or unrolling in appearance.

Virgo Symbol: This symbol mostly has variants of the cross of matter; with the V-like shape; though, there is an odd representation of the soul's crescent. The Greek version of the glyph (on the left) and its later (on the right) form are shown here.).

Libra Symbol: An unusual symbol, clearly reflecting ' The Scales ' traditionally associated with it, but also curious in its combination of the circle of spirit with the crescent of soul — forming an almost closed circle; this portion of the symbol is then positioned above parallel horizontal lines — more indicating a distinction from matter above and below.

Scorpio Symbol: A couple of different forms of the Scorpio glyph are shown here, both of which display the cross of matter as very prominent and pointing upward, with an arrow tip, as in the symbol for Mars. Maybe we can see some kind of angular soul crescent in the "M" type. For my job, I prefer to use the left glyph, because I like the coiled and almost spring-like feeling: The Scorpion.

Sagittarius Symbol: Here are two types of the cross of matter, both of which share a true sense of direction. Of course, this is the Archer, but apart from that, the key here is directionality — getting to the point.

Capricorn Symbol: Capricorn is a strange mixture of the soul's crescent and the cross of matter, along with a few curves of the 'crescent of soul.' This reflects the Goat, but in and of itself is a fascinating concept.

Aquarius Symbol: Here, we mostly have variations on the soul's crescent, giving a sense of waves and water that goes with Aquarius, the Water Carrier.

Pisces symbol: Two Pisces types, the Greek one on the left and the more modern version on the right. Both have clearly shown the crescent of the spirit, and in duplicate. The cross of the matter is only seen in the version on the right.

CHAPTER TEN:

How Astrology Can Be Used To Predict The Future

Some astrological forecasts do not include an individual's predictions. For example, some astrologers are making predictions for businesses.

This is achieved in almost the same manner as an individual's prediction; instead of using a person's birth chart, the chart of the period that the corporation was formed or became a legal entity in some other form is used. Many astrologers make predictions for countries or other areas that are politically specified. This is often accomplished by examining the time chart when the nation or city became a legally independent entity.

There are also occasions where maps of major political figures are used as they can affect the fate of the nation or other geographic areas they control. Certain types of forecasts are weather projections or natural phenomena like earthquakes.

This method of prediction differs from predictions for individuals, companies and countries where no birth chart is involved; in general, the astrologer analyzes the positions of the planets in the sky, especially in critically important periods such as the New Moon, the Full Moon, or when the Sun enters a new zodiac sign. Many astrologers claim to be able to forecast specific events in the future; this is a fairly common practice in Vedic astrology, for example.

Nevertheless, most Western astrologers only talk of patterns and not specific events. For instance, an astrologer will predict that you are likely to attract unpredictable events into your life over a certain period of time and there is a good chance that you will get into an accident, but this can be avoided by being extra careful.

Many astrologers believe that individuals with varying degrees of success can handle the astrological influences and it is up to the imagination of the individual and the free will of the person to decide the ultimate outcome of how the astrological influence will manifest itself. The movements of the planets around the zodiac set off angles to stations where planets were when a person is born, and when they do that, things are liable to happen to that person. There are orders to how transports work.

There are several possibilities for each transport because they can work in different ways, depending on the context of a person's birth chart, and the chapter in the person's life so be sure to check everything before making that prediction. It's an easy mistake for an apprentice and even some certified astrologers. For example, Uranus in combination with the birth chart of Venus will not create a love affair in the horoscope of a two-year-old nor will Jupiter in the mid-heaven of a homeless drug addict unexpectedly show "advancement in his profession.

Another common mistake a person could make is to try to make a prediction based on just one factor alone; you need to look at all of them because you just can't tell, that Jupiter aspect you've been counting on to increase your money may be cancelled by the accident aspect between Uranus and Mars. Calculating the estimate of progressions is taken as equal to one year of your life every day after your birth.

For example, if you want to find a person's progression when the person was 20 years old, you would calculate a new horoscope for 20 days after the said person's birth date using the same year, same time of day, and even the same place of birth, to make up a 'Progressed Horoscope' 20-year-old. And note, when calculating progression estimates, the parts which are correct within one degree are the most influential part on a person at that period of time and even for a long period of time, so you need to establish that the Progressed Horoscope is correct within one degree. And you can do this by comparing your birth planets and your progressed planets to check for any differences between them. There are several approaches applied to use astrology to predict our future:

1. Transits Transit is basically predicting the future with "Transit elements." What are transiting elements? They are the day's cosmic location in the sky; they're the heavenly spots in the atmosphere for a day. So, to predict a person's future, you compare the planets' positions in the birth chart with the one in the sky. Assuming, Grace's natal Venus is at 10 degrees of Gemini and Jupiter transiting (now Jupiter's position) is also at 10 degrees of Gemini, then Jupiter transiting is Grace's natal Venus conjunct. Therefore, for Grace, it is a Jupiter-Venus day, a perfect day for people to enjoy, gatherings and just have a nice time to relax.

Some astrologers use midpoints while others use asteroids, almost all astrologers use transiting planets to aspects of the natal planet, and the vast majority of astrologers believe that transits across angles are very important, in other words, crossing the Descendants, Ascendants, or 4th house cusp. If I want to predict what is going to happen to a particular person today, then you equate the planets' positions in the sky today with the planets' positions in the birth chart of that person.

Some astrologers also look at transiting declines; that is, it is important to consider the time when a transiting planet has the same decline as a native planet. Now another important thing to know is about the calculated sidereal zodiac and the calculated tropical zodiac transits.

In the tropical Zodiac, the transiting elements are one degree earlier than the sidereal zodiac because of the amount of precession that had come up since the person was given birth to. Taking into account that precession is the tropical Zodiac's reverse passage through the sidereal Zodiac at a speed of one degree, if a person is about.

In addition to looking at features created by the transiting planets into the natal worlds, you will also be able to study the location of transiting planets in the houses of the birth chart. Many astrologers also match the zodiac signs of the transiting planets with the Zodiac signs of the natal planets, others are probably not the most understandable approach, they are clear and natural and almost instinctively happen.

2. The Monthly Moon Cycle People, in general, go through change, they move on, they marry, give birth, buy stuff, loose stuff. They do all the things they've always wanted to do; it's a moment when everything seems to happen to everyone at once.

People are filled with desire; emotions are high, they go out, some to party, some mingle, some get into a bar brawl, others prefer to go on a first date. Relationships are starting and ending or changing in some new way; people are irrational.

Each month, you normally have one and sometimes two Full Moons which is known as the Blue Moon. You can learn what kind of energy the Full Moon is going to produce by being centred on the sign-in which the Full Moon is. The cycles between the New Moon and the Full Moon are imaginative, and the periods between the Full Moon and the new are less creative, even confusing at times and that is why each month, all of these cycles are unpredictable.

The New Moon often provides a way for people to anticipate how they behave. They sometimes feel like withdrawing, pulling away to focus and communicate with their spiritual truth in order to come up with the idea that they will cultivate up to the Full Moon to help them reach their target. People tend to feel sleepy and stay in.

3. Saturn Returns

The Saturn Return is a major transition in life that happens to most people. Saturn is a planet of time and duty. A Saturn return is when Saturn comes back to the same point when a person is born, and this usually takes place around the age of 29.

People usually go through some sort of existential defining moment and at this moment, they tend to change their life and fundamental beliefs, jolting their foundation. This is a rite of passage, of sorts, where we grow and have a much deeper level of knowledge of our life purpose, of our objectives. It may be taxing, but the good news is that this diminutive death is also a rebirth that helps us to grow and connect to life at a deeper and much fulfilling level. And if we find it too demanding and try to ignore our higher calling, we're going to go through a soul-awakening experience that will stir us up to it.

4. Solar Return Charts

Solar Return charts are snapshots of the skies as the Sun returns to its natal placement or where it was when you were born, in a given year. Solar Return Charts are estimated for precise time the Sun returns to its place of creation, that is, within two days of birthday. Such maps can be interpreted much like natal charts, except the fact that they are in place only for one year (from birthday to birthday) should be considered. You will read as much information as you want on a Solar Return page. Several important points to consider in reading Solar Return Charts are as follows; The Solar Return Chart's

Ascendant will colour the approach of the person to the year's setting.

For example, if in the Solar Return chart Aries is on the Ascendant, with increased energy and enthusiasm, and perhaps with some impatience, the individual would approach the year. The ruler of the Ascending Sign will hold more knowledge about the general disposition and emphasis of the person, and their place by sign, home, and aspect. Remember the planets and points are actually brought to an angle of the Solar Return map in the natal table, if any.

For instance, let's say the Solar Return Ascendant is Virgo 22 degrees, and Venus' birth location is Virgo 24 degrees. The natal Venus is, therefore, the Solar Return Ascendant, and the state and issues surrounding the natal Venus of the person can be presumed highlighted in solar return year.

This analysis tells us what circumstances of birth or deep-rooted personality problems are highlighted in the Solar Return year. For instance, if you have a native Sun square Mars and the Sun is on the Solar Return Ascendant, perhaps with Mars on the Midheaven as well, we may safely assume that the Sun-Mars struggle or difficulty is demonstrated in a way that is both public (midheaven) and personal (ascendant). Remember likewise what Solar Return planets are at the angles of Solar Return.

These are transits that are accentuated in the Solar Return year. What's the Sun's condition? Where's the house located? Naturally, we know the sign because it's going to be in the same birth position. This may be a focus area for the coming year.

What are the aspects it makes? Where is the Moon located? The Moon's location by house and sign will indicate, so to speak, where your heart is. For example, if the Solar Return Moon is in the 5th house in Libra, you are likely to be emotionally attached to and focused on love and relationship. In this area of life, there will be more than easy variations within store if, for example, the Moon also forms a square to Pluto in the Solar Return table. Profound changes are likely to take place here.

Factoring in the elements of the Moon will thus help to improve the interpretation.

5. The Retrograde Cycles

When they go backwards, the inner planets of Mercury, Venus, Mars each have an expected effect. Mercury messes with electronics, mail and communication 3 times a year for 3-4 weeks at a time and it is common knowledge that this is when websites go down, computers crash, and people have trouble clearly communicating what they mean.

When Mercury stations lead, things can move forward like clockwork, and more so when the post-shadow period ends. We should expect ex-lovers to emerge or dream about them when Venus goes backwards. When Mars goes backwards, we can expect our sexual urges to lessen or our desire to decrease temporarily as our excitement sinks. There will be a change in others and in ourselves as these things happen consecutively.

So, when a computer in perfectly good shape suddenly crashes and connections are down, it's simply because the inner planets are messing with us. Or when a long-forgotten boyfriend unexpectedly calls, Mercury is leading!

6. Locate the Inner Planets Our month's theme and the general manner in which people act and sound can be determined by what the Sun is in. It can be calculated by looking at what sign the Moon is in, the everyday emotional atmosphere and the energy available to you and to others. Over 30 days, the Sun remains in one sign, and the Moon stays in 2.5. When you know the planetary energies and sign characteristics, you will begin to predict how the inner planets in a sign will influence people's general mood and yourself.

If you're interested in learning where each planet is going to be, you can use an ephemeris that gives data on which sign each planet is every day. Of note, outer planets also have a major impact on us. Jupiter, Saturn, Neptune, Uranus, and Pluto have longer cycles producing stable environments on the world's small as well as large scale.

7. Horoscopes. You will read your horoscopes regular, weekly, monthly and annual to recognize the trends and energies you are going to deal with during those periods. Reviewing your horoscope can help you see how these themes play out before, during and after certain transits.

In fact, reading the horoscope for your Rising Sign may be more valuable rather than your sun sign, and many astrologers accept this as the truth.

8. Eclipse Season. One prediction you can always make is that there will be major changes in life in the people around us, our own lives and core values structures every year during the two eclipse seasons.

Eclipses normally occur over the span of one or two months, and new homes, new jobs, new relationships and many major life decisions come with them. People often don't know its eclipse season, and they're shocked to see these changes happening for everyone at once. When you watch your own mental process, it can be very beneficial if the changes don't catch you off guard.

As these events hit, you can even sense the build-up of electricity. A solar eclipse's energy means the Sun's energy is moving us forward. We can use our attention to reflect on just what our goal is so that the Sun drives us to our targets rather than just being pulled.

9. Returns to the Moon. Many astrologers use the lunar return map that takes place about once a month to forecast the coming month. Many astrologers believe that the lunar return chart especially affects moon-ruled matters such as moods, home life, etc.

10. Other Returns (Mercury, Mars, Jupiter, Saturn and Neptune) Some astrologers analyze the returns of Mercury (the time Mercury returns to its native position), the returns of Venus, Mars, etc. These returns are referred to as planetary returns sometimes, to differentiate them from the more commonly known solar and lunar returns. Because the planets can turn back, a planetary return can occur many times in a

relatively short period as the planets retrograde over the natal position.

Usually, for example, returns from Mercury and Venus occur either once a year or three times a year. For example, if Mercury retrogrades over the natal Mercury's position, thus making a second return to Mercury, it must eventually turn direct and cross this position a third time. For the other planets, the same is true.

Mars will return to her birthplace for about 2 1/2 years, Jupiter every 12 years, Saturn every 29 1/2 years, Uranus every 7 years, Neptune every 14 years, and Pluto every 21 years. In some cases, it may be impossible to calculate the exact time of a planetary return! The reason this is an issue is that the slower the earth, the more precise the measurements will have to be to determine the exact moment of the return.

The biggest problem happens when the planet becomes retrograde or direct as the earth seems to travel very, very slowly at this time. When a planet changes direction from forward to retrograde, or retrograde to forward, it is called stationary because it does not move at all for a second, and it moves extremely slowly for a while around this moment.

The slower a world moves, the harder it is to assess when the return takes place. If a planet is at a po at the time of return, it is impossible to determine the time of the return with great accuracy. Most astrologers prefer "half returns" or "quarter returns" as well. A half-return occurs when the planet returns its native position to the point of opposition; for instance, about halfway between two birthdays, the Sun reaches a point where its native position is opposed. It takes around 84 years for Uranus to return to his birthplace, and Neptune and Pluto are even slower so that astrologers generally do not use outer planet returns. Few astrologers make use of planetary returns.

Another approach is the Sun Return Chart. The Sun Return Map is another solution. Twice a year, once on your birthday, and again, six months later on your "half-birthday," you can improve every part of your life. The sun "returns" every year to the degree it occupied when you were born. The horoscope for that specific time and place is called the Sun Return Chart and it impacts you for the next year.

However, most of the effect occurs in the first six months. You have your "Half-Solar Return Chart" six months later, and that has an impact on the last half of your personal year. If you don't like them, the nice thing about these return charts is that you can change them. Like any horoscope, you have to schedule these return charts for a location as well as a date, you can't change your birthday or half-birthday period, but you can choose where to be at that moment.

When you travel, the chart wheel turns, and the house positions of the planets change. More importantly, the horoscope angle aspects (Ascendant and Mid-Heaven) are changing. The angles are very important. They show the points we make contact with the outside world, how we start things. Its where the rubber horoscope meets the road. And for the return charts, when we travel, Angles will change.

One of my favourite movements is to position Jupiter, the planet of expansion and "luck" in the second house (money) and have the Mid-Heaven (job) trine (120 degrees, a "lucky" angle). After all, if you want to better your career, you could get paid for it as well. Oh yes, before we get going, one really important thing, the orbit of the Moon wobbles around the Sun.

Because of this procession, the Sun takes a little longer each year to return to the position it occupied at your birth (yes, of course, it is the Moon that passes around the Sun, but since we live on earth, horoscopes are set up geocentrically). To get a similar horoscope, we need to repair this. And to make sure you're checking the solar return maps you're using. In practice, this means the position of the Sun is going to be a little more than on your birth chart. And every year the change gets bigger. Finally, everybody's birthday comes out a day later because of this correction of the procession. At the very beginning, I have to warn you that this view is controversial among astrologers. I use the Tropical Zodiac, but the correction of precession is a sidereal astrology technique. This is not a combination of apples and oranges? What am I allowed to say? Everything functions.

And since I have six earth signs on stars, that's the bottom line for me. I gave a lecture at an NCGR conference in December 1997 comparing the corrected charts with those that were not corrected. They have given similar results on several occasions. However, the precession corrected return horoscope gained hands down whenever they gave different answers.

Making Sense of the Transit Listings

Example of transit-to-natal aspects is:

June 1: Sun trine Jupiter. June 3: Merc Sqr Ura Ven conj Sat June 4: Plus, opp Sun This listing shows that on June 1 the transiting Sun will be tried to birth Jupiter. Astrologers usually mention the transiting planet first and the natal planet second when relating to a transiting planet to the dimension of the natal planet.

Many astrologers would say this individual will have opportunities for progress on June 1 or at least enjoyable activities and contacts on June 1. Note that nothing is mentioned on June 2 in this report. On a few days, there will be more transiting effects on other days. Naturally, how many aspects one uses depends on the number of transiting planets to natal planet aspects.

The key aspects (conjunction, opposition, line, trine, sextile, and quincunx) are used in this sample listing, and there are no aspects on some days. On June 3, there are two things in this sample listing: the transiting Mercury is the square natal Uranus, and the transiting Venus is the Saturn conjunct. One thing happens on June 4: transiting Pluto is the native Sun of opposition.

For the obvious reason they move through a larger zodiac period, offering them more opportunities, the fast-moving planets such as Sun, Mercury, and Venus make more aspects than the slow moving planets, such as Uranus, Neptune, and Pluto to look at the natal planets.

The transiting Moon moves much faster than the other body, and it forms numerous aspects of the natal chart that the majority astrologers ignore the transiting Moon except when they study a specific period of a few hours or less in detail. There are very few aspects to the slower moving planets, but when they do, they have a stronger impact on the person than the transits of the inner planet.

For the clear reason, they pass a larger zodiac period to give them more opportunity to the rapidly moving planets of the Sun, Mercury and Venus than the slow moving planets of Uranus, Neptune and Pluto. Therefore, the long-lasting transits of the outer planet will make major changes in the life of a person.

Probably the vast majority of astrologers agree that the inner planets are more personal, so that the transit of the outer planet to the inner planet is an extremely powerful influence, for example when the transiting Uranus (or Neptune or Pluto) is square (or any other major aspect of the natal Moon) The effect on the person (or Sun, Mercury, Venus, Mars) is extremely powerful.

Similarly, if Saturn is in Gemini at 25 degrees, I can look in my birth chart to see where Saturn would fall in terms of the house position. If my 3rd house contains that degree of Gemini, then I would know that Saturn is transiting through my 3rd house. Now showing relationships between planets and love.

Taking LOVE as a case study. Love can be unpredictable! An annual love horoscope will give you a glimpse of the headed romantic energies, but the story is so much more! This is because your unique astrological design has a tremendous effect on how certain cosmic events affect your love life. Your Big Picture 1-Year Astrology Love Forecast blends your personal astrology with the long-term astrological cycles and big planetary transits you choose over the 12-month timeframe.

The study details the peak days of each of your romantic periods, so you will know when those forces are having the greatest effect on your love potential. . In your annual love astrology forecast, the following chapters are included: Your Sign of Love. How do you want to love your Sun sign? This section of the report answers this question, providing you with a better understanding of the show patterns of your sign as well as a summary of the year in love for your sign.

The Moon may have a major impact on your romantic mindset! This chapter highlights the importance of specific cycles of New Moon and Full Moon, helping you to gage in love your instinctive, gut-level needs, allowing you to maximize your potential in any relationship over the coming year. Your Love Cycles, Venus, are among the most important influences on your love cycles. It is your ability not only to attract and receive lovers!

Knowing how the transits of Venus affect your natal planets gives you the most positive way to manifest love. Your Sexual Energy Mars is the initiation, inspiration, and driving world— but did you know that your sexual and impulsive energy is also controlling it? Pinpointing how the transits of Mars fuel your birth chart not only shows you when this energy will increase for you but also how you can make the most of it!

Once Jupiter attaches in your birth chart to a planet, it opens up possibilities in every aspect of your life.— including heart issues! Practical love Well, so Saturn isn't heaven's most love-dopey world, but that doesn't mean it doesn't matter when it comes to romance! This planet knows one or two things about endurance, so understanding when it touches your chart gives you the opportunity to snag your expected commitment.

Revolutionary love

There's a reason why Uranus is called the "Great Awakener" — this planet loves sudden and dramatic change. Bracing for the impact of Uranus on your chart will help you embrace this revolutionary energy, enabling you to break free from traditional patterns and transform your life of love.

Blissful and Transformative Love

Don't let Neptune and Pluto's slow movement confuse you! Knowing Neptune's features on your chart allows you to work on the more spiritual side of love, while Pluto's movements provide insight into how to completely revamp your present romantic situation. In conclusion, you can get from an expert astrologer a migration, transition, or solar return reading to help you if you're trying to see what kinds of situations to plan for.

Such projections can still be used to help you develop and not just sit back and let life happen to you. Even with the insights that a master astrologer can make, they won't give us true happiness until we try to be a better person and take responsibility for our words, thoughts and actions.

Essentially, don't become overly dependent on projections; you might spend so much time predicting what's going to happen that you fail to manifest. Astrology's point is to find your talent first and see what your soul has come here to do to help the world. We use astrology to co-create the future as we use the Moon cycles to manifest the resources we need.

We can use the forecasts because we know our vulnerabilities to take the higher path, not be reactive, not get frustrated, and channel the strength to be friendly and helpful global citizens.

Predictions of astrology become a crutch when we're only looking for things like love and money to come to us. One of the Universe's higher laws states the energy we are sending out is what we are getting back.

That means that we have to concentrate on being a good person to meet other good people. In order to receive it, we must give energy. We can't just sit back and think that astrology will solve everything, we need to use our will to purify our intentions on a daily basis using the astrology tool to become the best and most friendly versions of ourselves as possible, that's what I consider'